The First President

The Rt Hon. Lord Horder of Ashford
G.C.V.O., M.D., D.C.L., F.R.C.P.

ANOTHER WAY

THE HORDER CENTRE
SIXTY YEARS OF EVOLUTION

Charles Gallannaugh

authorHOUSE®

AuthorHouse™ UK Ltd.
1663 Liberty Drive
Bloomington, IN 47403 USA
www.authorhouse.co.uk
Phone: 0800.197.4150

Published by AuthorHouse 06/03/2013

ISBN: 978-1-4817-9684-2 (sc)
ISBN: 978-1-4817-9680-4 (hc)
ISBN: 978-1-4817-9692-7 (e)

ACKNOWLEDGEMENTS

To that host of unsung heroes, who over the first 50 years of the Horder Centre valiantly struggled with their Imperial typewriters, assiduously reporting the activities that took place, recording them in the minutes of the committee meetings they attended, I am most grateful. Likewise those who transcribed the turgid prose emanating from those in high places who introduced the Acts of Governments with their associated edicts that were meant to guide the activities of lesser mortals, I express my thanks. Without these records, written and preserved over the years, the history of the Centre would have been based on individual recollection, a notoriously unreliable source, rather than facts as recorded at the time the events occurred and the work of those scribes carried out with much diligence and thoroughness deserves to be passed on down the years.

The idea of assembling the historical record of the Centre was that of the current Chief Executive Diane Thomas and her support and encouragement throughout has been constant and enthusiastic. At the time she put forward her proposal much of the archive was mislaid and only as the project developed did a great deal more come to light. Had she not taken the initiative when she did much might have been irrevocably lost.

Many people have been of great assistance in finding material that related to the task in hand. It would be impossible to mention all individually but I am grateful in particular to the following. The administrative staff of the Centre, Alison Green, Sophie Dubber, Teresa Kent, Jemma Smith and the marketing manager, Claire Powell, who helped me to unearth photographs and other records, have been most helpful throughout. Martin James did sterling work locating and transporting files, setting up an office where they could be stored more safely. Peter Deere whose father worked at the old Crowborough West Camp as a warrant officer in the army before it was purchased by the Marchioness introduced me to matters that might well have been lost had he not drawn my attention to them.

A number of friends gave freely of their time for which I am most grateful. Mrs Evelyn Zago and her friend Mrs Waltraud Griggs very kindly translated the article in the magazine of the German Red Cross described in the first chapter in the sketch of Cecilia Bochenek's early life. My lifelong friend Dr Ivor Slee and I spent a most enjoyable morning in London where he exercised his formidable skills, not this time as an anaesthetist but as a photographer, when we took pictures of the former homes of the Marchioness and Bochenek and visited St Bartholomew's Hospital, an occasion followed by an enjoyable lunch spent reminiscing together as has been our custom at intervals since our earliest days. John Ball the former Chief Executive of the Centre provided me with valuable material both verbal and documentary together with film footage taken in the very early years of the Centre's activity. Lene Gurney, whose nursing skills helped me to care for my patients over much of three decades, provided me with her memories of the first patient to be operated on at the Centre, with whom she had kept in touch for many years following his operation and showed me a cupboard that turned out to be a veritable treasure trove of historical data.

I am grateful to the archivist at St Bartholomew's Hospital who allowed me to use the Nicholson portrait of the late Lord Horder as I am to Rebecca Holmes and Sue Croucher of the Education Trust of my old school Epsom College who provided information and the photograph of the former Old Epsomian and Horder Centre Chairman the late Denys Milne CBE. Librarians at the East Sussex Record Office and the Royal Society of Medicine could not have been more helpful. Diana Manipud of the Liddell Hart Centre at King's College London Archive went to great trouble to find me photographs of the bomb-damaged St Thomas' Hospital. Where I have consulted other works and referred to them in the text a reference is provided at the end of each chapter to assist those who wish to undertake more detailed study.

To three people who have assisted me greatly I owe particular thanks. Professor Malcolm Forsythe provided advice and comment that has prevented me from committing errors of judgement best avoided. His agreement to write the foreword to this history of the Horder Centre, with which he has been so closely associated, was a kindness much appreciated by his old friend. My daughter Diana brought her former professional editing expertise to bear on the text giving up her free time in spite of pursuing a busy career nowadays as a nurse. Her skills have prevented me from committing avoidable errors of syntax but where errors or the occasional solecism occur in spite of her wise advice it is entirely the result of my own ineptitude.

Finally to my wife Gillian who has encouraged and cajoled when energy was flagging, accepted with equanimity outbursts of displeasure aimed at the electronic wizardry now used for writing in place of the quill pen and who has provided the necessary stimulant for the ageing brain when required, I express my love and gratitude.

FOREWORD

The evolution of The Horder Centre in its first 50 years has vividly demonstrated the risks that can occur when trying to cater for selected chronic diseases. The early ambition to have a purpose-built facility, which those severely disabled by rheumatoid arthritis could call their home, was shattered with the introduction of new and highly successful drugs such as steroids. This occurred very early on in its history and meant that some very radical thinking had to be done by The Horder Committee of Management in order to find a new purpose.

What emerged was something that defied all contemporary thoughts as to how clinical care should be provided. The concept in 1962 of a District General Hospital (DGH) was that it had a facility in which all the specialties worked and interacted to address 'common conditions which commonly occurred' within its catchment population. Single specialty hospitals whether for Eyes, ENT or Orthopaedics or other solitary specialties closed all over the country as their services were transferred.

Improved access both in distance to travel and waiting time for treatment became increasingly important. What was fascinating, in the 1970s, was the way many elderly patients in Kent and Sussex awaiting hip replacement, with a wait of up to two years or more at their local DGH, declined offers of almost instant treatment in the London Teaching Hospitals where waiting times were minimal. Being closer to home and family was of paramount importance.

The idea, therefore, of seeking public funds and support for a single operating theatre to do joint replacements at a remote facility on the edge of a town in the Ashdown Forest, where the excellent local community hospital was already equipped with an under-used theatre, initially seemed absurd.

The waiting list problem was so serious that it became, and still is, a political expedient. Therefore the proposal from The Horder Centre had to be given careful thought by the National Health Service (NHS). The concept of the orthopaedic/anaesthetic team from surrounding DGHs bringing their own NHS patients to use the facilities of The Horder Centre offered a seamless pattern of care. However this, on its own, would not have been enough to guarantee a long-term future. There had to be such rigorous attention to quality that it would make general practitioners, and then the public, realise that this service was both efficient and effective.

So the 4-year project at The Horder Centre began and it has never looked back. It has been a salvation for the NHS orthopaedic services in the South East of England. We should all be grateful that Charles Gallannaugh, one of the key players in this success story, has documented all this within this book. It has indeed been Another Way.

Recent findings by Dr Foster, coupled with the award by Laing and Buisson of third prize in the Best Independent Hospitals list in 2012, give us grounds for optimism for the next 50 years.

Malcolm Forsythe   October 2012

INTRODUCTION

To use the word maverick to describe a middle-aged woman struck down in childhood by a cruel disease so that she was confined to a wheelchair would at first sight appear to be inappropriate. However, its definition as one who dissents from the accepted normal rules and pursues an independent line of thought to overcome apparently overwhelming odds, does suggest that maverick is a suitable word to describe Cecilia Bochenek who first introduced the concept that developed into the Horder Healthcare of today.

It is the purpose of this small book to show how, using Cecilia Bochenek's own words "a very badly crippled arthritic dedicated her life to help others with the same complaint". The inspiration that drove her did indeed at the time she introduced her ideas for the Centre, introduce a new approach to the way health care was provided for patients with advanced arthritis. To understand her motivation and those of the many people who worked so hard in the early days to set up the Centre, not long after a devastating war had destroyed much of continental Europe where she had been born and at a time when resources were scarce, it is useful perhaps to learn more about the way in which it evolved. The history of the Horder Centre provides insight into the ideas that inspired its founders, describes the way they went about their task and acts as a guide to the times when others came along with new initiatives to carry forward the ideals that they had envisaged.

Fortunately many of the early records of the Horder Centres for Arthritics, as the organisation was first called, have been preserved and much that follows here is based on a study of these. A number of key figures in the story, because they are well known, have been the subject of comment elsewhere and, where appropriate, reference has been made to this. Most importantly there are some still around who remember those early days and their recollections are both fascinating and enlightening.

The story of the Horder Centre falls conveniently into two parts. The first part describes the time from its founding until the death of Cecilia Bochenek in 1981. The second part describes the establishment of the surgical unit and the development of a modern joint replacement service. A final chapter outlines the major developments that have taken place there in the early twenty-first century and that continue to this day. Through much of the narrative I have referred to the two principal figures by their surnames only, not to imply any form of disrespect, but to avoid tiresome repetition. Where the cost of important activities is given, the figures shown are not the contemporary ones but the amount corrected for inflation in 2012.

The purpose of recounting history is to put before the reader facts enabling him to learn about what happened in the past and thus be guided in the future. An interpretation of the facts by the author is also called for and responsibility for this must be taken by him as it is here. If that leads to controversy so be it, but the expectation must be that from such debate will result future benefit. It is hoped that patients, who often ask how the Centre came into being, will find this account of interest and will discover how the practice of medicine has evolved rapidly over the past half century, from what might be regarded as quite old-fashioned beginnings into the age of technology in which their current treatment takes place. Whether the art of medicine as currently practised has lost something on the way, or perhaps gained something as it has embraced science, I leave the reader to decide.

TABLE OF CONTENTS

PART 1
1952 – 1981
AN IDEA BECOMES REALITY

PART 2
1981 – 2011
THE INTRODUCTION OF SURGERY

PART 1

1952 – 1981

AN IDEA BECOMES REALITY

There is a tide in the affairs of women
Which, taken at the flood, – leads God knows where:
Byron. Don Juan; Canto VI

CHRONOLOGY 1952 – 1981

1948 – National Health Service Act introduced on 5 July. Regional Hospital Boards, Local Health Authorities and Boards of Governors of Teaching Hospitals established.

1952 – Cecilia Bochenek starts to record the names of founding shareholders using the name "Recuperative Homes for Arthritics".

1954 – Lord Horder GCVO, MD, DCL, FRCP becomes first President.

1954 – The Horder Centres for Arthritics registered with the LCC by Cecilia Bochenek and Dr Joyce Peake. Announcement in London newspapers Public Notices, 1 December.

1954 – Earliest surviving record of a meeting of the committee of management dated 6 December.

1955 – Edwina, Countess Mountbatten of Burma CI, GBE, DCVO becomes the second President following the death of Lord Horder.

1955 – Philip Shephard Esq. appointed first Chairman with Cecilia Bochenek Honorary Secretary.

1956 – The Golden Book launched to record names of leading financial donors.

1957 – Establishment of the first group of Horder Centres Helpers in Thorpe, Norwich.

1958 – Aims of the organisation defined for the first time in the Annual Report.

1959 – Maureen, Marchioness of Dufferin and Ava joins the committee.

1960 – Death of Countess Mountbatten of Burma, recorded in the minutes of the committee held on 25 Feb 1960 at Hans Crescent.

1960 – HRH Princess Margaret becomes the third President.

1960 – Purchase of the former Crowborough West Camp by the Marchioness of Dufferin and Ava from the Secretary of State for War.

1961 – Horder Centre registered as a charity under the new Charities Act 1960.

1962 – Building of the Centre at Crowborough begins on 4 June.

1962 – Bochenek and Peake move to the bungalow at Crowborough, the first building on site.

1963 – Transfer of parcel of land at Crowborough by Deed of Gift to the Charity by the Marchioness of Dufferin and Ava.

1966 – Resignation of Marchioness and other members of the committee. Dr Joyce Peake becomes first Medical Director.

1966 – Official opening of the Horder Centre in Crowborough on 27 October by HRH Princess Margaret following admission of the first patients.

1971 – Second phase of building starts.

1972 – Visit of HRH Princess Margaret to view new buildings.

1974 – NHS re-organisation. Regional Health Authorities, Area Health Authorities and District Management Teams established.

1974 – Award of MBE to Cecilia Dorothea Bochenek.

1977 – Visit by Secretary of State for Health, David Ennals, following adverse report by local Community Health Council.

1980 – Discussions regarding proposal to build an operating theatre and undertake surgery at the Centre. Decision taken in December to abandon this proposal.

1981 – Death of Cecilia Dorothea Bochenek MBE on 22 April.

ILLUSTRATIONS AND LEGENDS PART 1

THE FOUNDERS AND THE NAME

On the 1 December 1954 a Public Notice appeared in a London newspaper announcing an application for the registration with the London County Council of The Horder Centres for Arthritics. The National Health Service (NHS) had come into being just over 6 years before and it had already become apparent that those who had established this new system of health care, intended to be free at the point of delivery, had not anticipated the difficulties of providing for the chronic sick, disabled and elderly in a service where demand would always exceed the available resources. The 'man on the Clapham omnibus' to evoke the perceptive idiom of the late Lord Denning may have welcomed the opportunity to benefit from the so-called free service although he was to pay heavily for it in his taxes. However those who could not get on the omnibus because of disability or chronic illness were already being left behind.

It was in this environment that Cecilia Bochenek, known by her friends as Cilla, decided to pioneer a plan that had first formed in her mind many years before. Born in Frankfurt Am Main in Germany on the 2 March 1906, with German, Polish, Czech and Russian grandparents, at the age of six she had developed juvenile rheumatoid arthritis or Still's Disease. Subjected to palliative care, which was the only help available to her and her parents at that time, she eventually realised that if she was to make anything of her life she would have to call upon her own resources. She travelled to England from Germany in 1927, after training as a teacher at Berlin University, with the intention of staying for 6 months to perfect her language skills. She worked in a boarding school on the east coast, which she enjoyed and later took a part-time teaching post at St James's Secretarial College near Hyde Park Corner. Sadly she had to give this up eventually as the physical effort of getting to work was too much for her. However she decided to stay in England and apparently continued to tutor in history, geography and languages at her home in West Kensington.

She often told the story to journalists who interviewed her for magazine or newspaper articles of how she had been told "We can do nothing more for you. Now it is up to you". She described her approach to managing her illness in a short article in the 1958 *Report of The Horder Centres* and it provides insight into the driving force which motivated many of her later actions. She wrote "It was realised that such patients, unless helped in a special way, often became quite reconciled to depend upon others and more than willing to be waited upon hand and foot. This outlook is by no means the result of anything lacking in the treatment, nor should the patient be blamed for it. His illness taught him life must be difficult and painful, but he has not been shown to what extent he can, by his own effort, still take his place in the community". Such an enlightened approach was uncommon at that time and is as relevant to the care of those with chronic disability today as it was then.

Although Bochenek had been contemplating for many years the idea of establishing residential homes for arthritics, to use the somewhat archaic

contemporary term, according to an interview she gave in the 1970s that was printed in the magazine of the German Red Cross, the idea that was to give rise to the Horder Centre came to her during a stay of 3 months in hospital after she tripped over a rug in her home in London. The precise date of this accident is not recorded although evidence suggests that it was in the late 1940s. Following this event she became virtually housebound. It appears that it was shortly after this, almost certainly around 1952, that she decided to approach Lord Horder with her ideas. She had little in the way of contacts or financial resources but she resolved to establish residential centres where people with arthritis could be encouraged and helped to overcome their disabilities. Specially trained staff would teach them to adapt in such a way that they could become employed again or at least regain their dignity and independence. Her original idea was to establish a number of Centres throughout the country, but in practice her vision was to be embodied in what today is The Horder Centre at Crowborough in East Sussex, hereafter referred to as the Centre. In 1974 she was awarded the MBE in the New Year Honours in recognition of her achievement and she received her much-deserved award at Buckingham Palace from Queen Elizabeth the Queen Mother on 5 February 1974. In a photograph taken on that day she is seen with her brother, Artur Bochenek, and Dr Joyce Peake in the courtyard of the palace.

Bochenek had been assisted and supported in her endeavours by her friend Dr Dulce Joyce Peake. Born in 1902 in Battle, East Sussex, she was

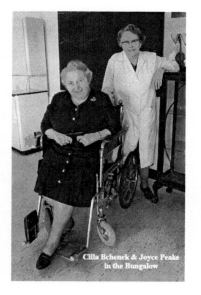
Cilla Bchenek & Joyce Peake in the Bungalow

one of the early women graduates in medicine, qualifying with the conjoint diploma MRCS, LRCP, at a time when women were rarely found in the profession. She had worked as a general practitioner in Wembley but in due course she gave up her practice and moved to join her friend. They lived in a flat at 17 Rugby Mansions in West Kensington where Joyce Peake continued to see private patients and it was at that address that the first committee meetings were held as the project evolved. Later, when the buildings at Crowborough were built in the 1960s, they moved to a bungalow, Panorama, one of the first buildings to be completed on site in December 1962. It is not clear how or when Peake first met Cecilia Bochenek but it seems likely that she could have been her doctor in London. From the time of the Centre's foundation she worked loyally in support of her friend, eventually outliving her. She died at the Centre on 21 May 1990 aged 89 and is buried at St John's Church nearby. An early exponent of the holistic approach to patient care she had become the Centre's first medical director in 1966, remaining in post until she retired somewhat belatedly in 1982.

When Bochenek and Peake decided to launch their scheme, Bochenek, not without some trepidation as she admitted, wrote to Lord Horder to ask for his support. Somewhat to her surprise, according to an article written by Peake that was published in *The Lancet* in April 1963, Lord Horder arranged for his secretary to telephone and make an appointment for them to see him in his consulting rooms. After listening to them he encouraged Bochenek to put her plans into action.

Thomas Jeeves Horder, who became the Rt Hon Lord Horder GCVO, MD, DCL, FRCP, was one of the foremost physicians in the land. Born in 1871 in Shaftesbury, Dorset, the son of a draper, he was educated at the local High School in Swindon to where the family had moved and St Bartholomew's Hospital (Barts), London. Appointed Physician in Ordinary to King Edward VII, George V, King Edward VIII, King George VI and Queen Elizabeth II, he counted three prime ministers amongst his patients along with many other prominent figures in society. After retirement from his post as senior physician at Barts, he served on many government committees both during and after the war and at the time of his death was chairman or president of seven organisations in addition to the Horder Centres, including the British Association of Physical Medicine. When Horder became a baron in 1933, the first Barts physician to be so honoured, his colleagues gave him an illuminated address which he treasured and kept until he died. On his retirement in 1936, the Governors of the hospital commissioned Sir William Nicholson to paint a portrait in his honour, which still hangs in his old hospital.

It is interesting to speculate why Lord Horder accepted Bochenek's request to help them with their idea

From the portrait by Sir William Nicholson.
Courtesy of St Bartholomew's Hospital Archives

and become the Centre's first President. When the NHS was introduced he had objected to many of the proposals put forward by Aneurin Bevan believing that they would destroy the relationship between doctor and patient.

Lord Horder and Lord Moran, Churchill's doctor, were the two medical titans of that time. They stood for election to the Presidency of the Royal College of Physicians three times, battles which Moran won although only by six votes on the last occasion. The tussles between them during the debates in the House of Lords are well described by Michael Foot in his 1973 biography of Bevan. Foot described Horder as a " ... a growling conscientious objector to almost any national health service in any form whatever".[1] Moran, known as "Corkscrew Charlie" in the profession, a sobriquet said by some to relate to his fund-raising skills and by others, less kindly perhaps, to his political gyrations during the gestation of the NHS, believed that once the Bill had been introduced the doctors would do their best to support it. According to Foot, Horder thought otherwise. "The Lords debates were chiefly notable for a renewed round in the all-in wrestling match between Lord Moran and Lord Horder." Moran "could not mollify Lord Horder. Horder admitted that the Minister 'has courage, enthusiasm, a nimble mind and I believe a conscientious belief that these proposals are in the best interests of the community. I think that the Minister will go far, but in what direction I am unable to say' ".[2]

In the end maybe both were right. The profession did indeed support the Bill and for the next 20 years or so those who had worked in the health sector in times before the introduction of the NHS continued to administer the clinical care they had been accustomed to provide. Gradually however as financial demands rose in response to developing scientific and pharmaceutical advances and the old traditions of the medical and nursing professions changed, not necessarily for the better, the forebodings expressed by Lord Horder are seen perhaps to have been justified. The hope now therefore must be that an ethos of skilled and compassionate patient care can be preserved in an era of scientific change and deep economic turmoil which was never envisaged when the NHS began. Such is the mission of the contemporary Horder Centre.

Bochenek recounted that when she approached Lord Horder asking him to accept the Presidency of her rudimentary organisation (one of her most important early decisions according to the Marchioness of Dufferin and Ava writing in 1995), he accepted, informing her that the idea was not only valuable but original because "nothing like it had been applied in Britain or any other country". He suggested she form a committee to formulate plans for Centres where people with arthritis could be taught to become independent. The concept of a Centre along these lines, but outside the confines of the NHS, would no doubt have appealed to him. He had a keen interest in arthritis and in 1936 he and Dr William Copeman, later to become a vice-president of the Horder Centres, had founded the Empire Rheumatism Council, renamed later the Arthritis and Rheumatism Council. Lord Porritt, in his foreword to the informative book by Kersley and Glyn on the history of rheumatology and rehabilitation, acknowledged Lord Horder as "the power behind the throne in the formation of rheumatology as a respectable specialty and, through the British Association of Physical Medicine, also of rehabilitation".[3] It may have been a combination of his doubts about the NHS and his interest in arthritis that led him to respond in the affirmative to Cecilia Bochenek's request.

Lord Horder did more than just allow his name to go forward. In addition to moral support he gave advice and helped with fund raising. In June 1955, with his backing, a concert was given at the Albert Hall by Dame Irene Kohler and raised £1200*. Gardening was his passion in retirement, and in 1955 he opened his large garden at Ashwood Chace near Petersfield in Hampshire with the aim of raising money for the Centres. Sadly he died suddenly from a coronary thrombosis aged 84 on 13 August 1955 at his home and he and his wife Geraldine are commemorated in the churchyard at Steep nearby.[4] According to newspapers at the time, he left no will, the administration of his estate passing to his son. Following his death a number of former colleagues who had asked him to help with patients or who had been patients of his themselves wrote of his kindness and compassion. One in particular, a Dr Megarry, responding to an obituary which had been published in the *British Medical Journal* described the character of the man: "He has come down, even on holiday, tearing himself away from his beloved garden to see patients for me, either for the most nominal of fees or

---

* In Part 1, and also in Part 2, the monetary figures shown, unless stated otherwise, are those of costs updated for inflation as at 2012.

for nothing at all. He was a great man, a beloved physician and the friend of kings who never lost the common touch."[5] The Horder Centre had lost a good and influential friend at an early stage.

Undaunted, Bochenek and Peake set about finding a new President. Meetings of the recently established committee took place and much energy was spent on fund raising with somewhat modest success. A number of eminent people were enrolled as vice-presidents whose principal function appears to have been to add gravitas to the organisation and thus attract

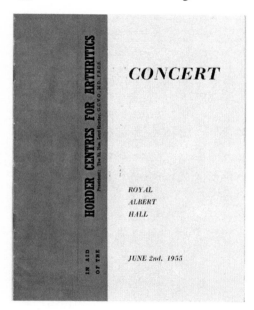

funds. Later, in 1966, the chairman Sir Edwin Leather questioned whether some of these people were taking an active interest or not and he wrote to a number of them to ask whether they wished to remain associated with the society. It seems that the number of vice-presidents was reduced following this initiative. An appeal for £1.2 million was announced by Bochenek in 1955 and reported in *The Daily Mail*. In an interview she said that this would enable an office to be set up, the first Centre to be built and a start to be made on the second. These Centres would be run more on home than hospital lines and be for patients who were not bed-ridden but were too disabled to be wage earners. They would stay in the Centre for 2-3 months and "learn how to become more independent". At that time, the newspaper cutting commented that "no area has been decided for the first Centre, which will house fifty patients". This early optimism was shortly to be exposed to the harsh realities of fund raising.

Bochenek often referred to herself as the sole founder. Whilst it is undoubtedly true that the original concept was hers, for which she should be given full credit as indeed the Marchioness of Dufferin and Ava did in her letter in 1995, a number of people were involved in its founding not least of whom was Dr Joyce Peake. The details of the original shareholders were recorded by Bochenek in a register in her own handwriting and it is noteworthy that she appears to have recruited them from 1952 onwards. The date of January 1955, when payment for the £1 share (£23 in 2012) was due, reflects no doubt the date when registration with the LCC, announced in the press in December 1954, became effective.

Founders as recorded in the Members and Share Ledger

Number	Name	Profession	Cash Due	Cash Paid
1	Norman Webber	Accountant	25.01.1955	16.06.1952
2	Peter Shepheard	Architect	25.01.1955	16.06.1952
3	FC Champneys	Solicitor	25.01.1955	16.06.1952
1	Miss E Lowe		25.01.1955	16.06.1952
2	Miss P McDonald		25.01.1955	16.06.1952
6	Mr W Vickers		25.01.1955	16.06.1952
7	Dr Joyce Peake	Medical Practitioner	25.01.1955	16.06.1952
8	Miss C Bochenek	Secretary	25.01.1955	16.06.1952
9	Philip Shephard	Printer	25.01.1955	03.12.1954
10	Miss Gray Ward		25.01.1955	03.12.1954
11	Mrs J Sandeman		25.01.1955	08.10.1954
12	Miss R Fawsett		25.01.1955	03.01.1954
13	EFJ Perkins		04.05.1955	04.05.1955

Philip Shephard was elected as the first chairman and Norman Webber was appointed treasurer, with Cecilia Bochenek as secretary. EFJ Perkins acquired and paid for his shareholding in May and after that no more shares were sold until 1959. Although he was not strictly speaking one of the 12 founders he can be grouped with them. He took over as chairman in January 1957 when Philip Shephard resigned.

The earliest record of a meeting of the committee of management to have been found is that of the sixth meeting which took place on 6 December 1954 in Bochenek's flat at 17 Rugby Mansions. Reference was made to the fifth meeting, which had taken place there in September, but no record has been found of this or earlier meetings. Bochenek and Peake had visited Lord Horder in November of that year and he had apparently given them a free hand telling them he only wished to be consulted on medical and ethical matters. It is likely that they had first approached him in 1952 and then, acting on his advice, set up a committee, that being the year when they started to enrol the founder members. In a letter thanking a generous benefactor written in 1980 by Bochenek not long before her death, in which she invited him and his wife to visit the Centre, she wrote "I am sure you would be interested to see what has come out of our little charity in 1952"; 1952 was the year in which the Horder Centre came into being in concept if not in actuality.

At the meeting on 6 December 1954, Bochenek reported that the formalities for changing the name, as Lord Horder had advised, had been completed and they were now registered as The Horder Centres for Arthritics. She appears to have anticipated events with this announcement to the committee, as the application for registration was not announced in the press until 12 December and not ratified until January 1955. When Bochenek and Peake first planned the organisation, they had named it "Recuperative Homes for Arthritics", but they were now in the process of registering it under its new name with the LCC in line with the *War Charities Act 1940*. Their original plan was to build a number of centres around the country, hence the use of the plural in the title, but in the event only one Centre was built.

Further Reading

1. Aneurin Bevan by Michael Foot. Vol. 2 1945-1960. London: Davis-Poynter; 1973. p124

2. Ibid p158-9.

3. A Concise International History of Rheumatology and Rehabilitation by Kersley and Glyn. London: Royal Society of Medicine Services Ltd; 1991. p ix.

4. The Little Genius by Mervyn Horder. London: Duckworth & Co; 1966. p120.

5. Obituary. British Medical Journal; Sept 10 1955. p684.

THE COUNTESS AND
THE MARCHIONESS

The unexpected death of Lord Horder presented a problem for the committee. At a meeting on 28 September 1955 a minute's silence was observed in his memory. After some discussion it was decided to offer the presidency, out of courtesy, to Mervyn Horder, his son, but if he did not accept then to approach Countess Mountbatten of Burma who had shown great interest in the work and who had already opened her garden at Broadlands that August to help raise funds for the Centre. The new Baron Horder declined the offer and in due course, in February 1956, Bochenek

Edwina, Countess Mountbatten
of Burma CI, GBE, DCVO
1901 – 1960

informed the committee that Edwina, Countess Mountbatten of Burma, had graciously accepted the presidency. This announcement was received with acclamation by the members. She went on to announce that two eminent rheumatologists, Dr Copeman and Dr Fletcher and a psychologist Dr JR Rees had said they were willing to become vice-presidents.

The life of Edwina Ashley, who following her marriage to Lord Louis Mountbatten became Edwina, Countess Mountbatten of Burma and the last Vicereine of India, was one of contrasts. Her mother died when she was 10 and as a young woman her upbringing was strongly influenced by her maternal grandfather, Sir Ernest Cassel, the financial advisor and close friend of Edward VII. A goddaughter of the King, Edwina, with her vivacity and beauty, became one of the most remarkable women of her age. From her grandfather, one of the richest men in Europe, she inherited at the age of 20, £74 million in today's terms. Her great wealth and contacts with royalty, first through her grandfather and then her marriage, gave her the freedom to live as she wished and for the next 20 years of her life she did just that. She travelled widely, pursuing a hedonistic life style in the years between the wars and this together with her socialist political leanings led to conflict with some in the Establishment.

However, the outbreak of war in 1939 brought about a radical change in her way of life. With her Jewish background she reacted with horror to the evils of National Socialism in Europe. In 1939 she enrolled herself at Westminster Hospital and undertook a 6-month training course in nursing and joined the Women's Voluntary Services and the St John Ambulance Brigade, becoming its County President for London in November. In his biography of her extraordinary life, Richard Hough[1] wrote "The post had in the past been largely nominal. It was no longer to be so. Edwina no more believed in figureheads than in monarchs". Showing great personal courage, her work in the East End of London during the Blitz brought widespread acclaim. When her husband Lord Louis Mountbatten was appointed Supreme Commander in South East Asia he relied on her to help with the relief of suffering of those who had endured so much cruelty during the Japanese occupation. He could have found no one better to carry out the work, which she repeated when as the last Vicereine of India she cared for those whose lives had been torn apart by the riots that swept through the sub-continent at the time of partition.

In spite of failing health, towards the end of her life she became involved with numerous charities. It is possible that she met Lord Horder in his capacity as the Royal Physician, her husband Lord Mountbatten being a close friend and aide-de-camp of the Prince of Wales, later Edward VIII. It is more than likely that Bochenek had approached her directly to draw the attention of the Countess to her fund-raising activities for the Centre. Following the death of Lord Horder, Bochenek informed the committee that Countess Mountbatten "had shown great interest in the work", and this no doubt strongly influenced their decision to approach her to become the second President of the Centres. Another feature of her character which would have attracted Bochenek was her forthrightness. Among a few of her comments quoted by Hough in his biography are "Well he'll have to learn to look after himself" and "Everyone should have an equal chance in life".[2] It is easy to see how this would have appealed to Bochenek and how the motivation behind her grand plan would have appealed to the Countess.

At a meeting of the committee in September 1959 members were informed that Countess Mountbatten had indicated her wish to attend the annual general meeting scheduled for the 17 March 1960 if her overseas tour ended in time. It was not to be. She was determined to undertake a tour of the Far East although her failing health made this unwise. Her friends tried to persuade her not to go but she seemed unable to lessen the frenetic pace of her life and went anyway. On the 20 February 1960 in Jesselton in Northern Borneo when it was clear to all that she was far from well she insisted on carrying out her duties in the stifling heat of the Orient and was photographed at a hospital comforting a patient the day before she died. That same night she died in her sleep. At the annual general meeting of the Centre the chairman Mr Perkins expressed the sadness felt by all members of the committee, sorrow he felt sure was shared by all the Helpers and arthritic members and indeed by thousands of people in all parts of the world.

Establishing the committee.

The first meetings were held in Bochenek's flat at Rugby Mansions in Kensington and fund raising was the principal concern in the early years. Various people retired from the committee pleading lack of time and others joined. An appeals committee was initiated in October 1956. In January 1957 Mr Shephard retired along with Miss Gray-Ward

Rugby Mansions 2011

and at the next meeting a new chairman EFJ Perkins took the chair.

In November 1957 an approach was made by a Dr Laws of 13 Park Crescent W1, offering the use of her waiting room for evening meetings which took place every other month. This was considered to be much more convenient for present and future committee members as lack of space was becoming a problem at Rugby Mansions. The first meeting there took place in July 1958 when it was decided to hold meetings every month instead of every second month. Meetings appear to

Hans Crescent 2011

have been held regularly at Park Crescent from then on until Dr Laws retired in 1959 when they were moved to 4 Hans Crescent, Knightsbridge, the house of the Marchioness of Dufferin and Ava.

In May 1958 four new committee members were elected, Sir Hugh Dawson Bt, Edwin Leather MP, His Honour Judge John Maude QC and Sir Tom O'Brien MP. Judge Maude was the third husband of Maureen, Marchioness of Dufferin and Ava. He and the Marchioness were to play a most significant role in the future development of the Horder Centre.

Maureen Constance Guinness, one of three daughters of the Honourable Arthur Guinness and granddaughter of the Earl of Iveagh, was born in 1907 in Grosvenor Place in London into a wealthy aristocratic family. The three vivacious and beautiful girls were known in the 1920s in both Irish and London Society as the bright and beautiful young things or the Guinness flapper girls. Maureen and her parents lived a life of luxury mixing with leading society figures, politicians and royalty. Maureen was "waited on hand and foot, a practice that she made sure continued until her death" according to her granddaughter Ivana Lowell in her recent candid memoir on her own life.[3] Her colourful life featured in the gossip columns throughout much of the twentieth century.

In 1930 Maureen married her cousin Basil at St Margaret's, Westminster. Basil was the 4th Marquess of Dufferin and Ava whose great grandfather had been Viceroy of India, a curious coincidence in view of Countess Mountbatten's links with India and the Horder Centres. He inherited the title while they were still on honeymoon when his father was killed in an aeroplane crash. They lived at Clandeboye, a three thousand acre estate in County Down and when in London, just off Knightsbridge, in a large house which would feature later in the early history of the Centres. Basil having distinguished himself at Oxford was acknowledged as a brilliant diplomat and politician but when in 1945 he was killed in action whilst serving with the army in Burma, by a strange quirk of fate near the village of Ava, he left Maureen widowed with three young children. Their 3-year-old son, Sheridan, then became the fifth Marquess of Dufferin and Ava. In due course Maureen married again but in deference to her late husband's wishes, so she maintained, she kept her title and was always known as the Marchioness of Dufferin and Ava. Her second marriage to an army officer was short lived ending in divorce after 6 years but in 1955 she married her third husband Judge John Maude QC. He died in 1986.

The village of Ava in Burma 2010

Her eccentricities and her habit of throwing large parties at her London home became a feature of the social scene. According to Ivana Lowell she gave a coming out party at her house in Hans Crescent for her daughter who became a debutante in the same year as Princess Margaret,[4] and this contact with royalty may have enabled her to approach the Princess later and ask her to accept the Presidency of the Horder Centre.

The first mention of the Marchioness with regard to the Horder Centres is recorded in the minutes of a meeting held on 12 February 1959: "The

Maureen, Marchioness of
Dufferin and Ava 1907 - 1998

Marchioness of Dufferin and Ava was one who kindly offered to visit patients. Last week this lady called on us with her niece, Mrs Maclean. Both have offered to form a branch and in addition, Lady Dufferin has agreed to take on the chairmanship of the United London Groups of Horder Centres Helpers". The Marchioness had apparently responded to a letter published by Bochenek in *The Daily Telegraph* "in which we appealed for people to form or join branches of Horder Centres Helpers".

In March 1959 another letter appeared in *The Daily Telegraph* publicising the fact that the Marchioness was taking over the chairmanship of the United London Groups of Horder Centres Helpers. The committee members then decided to invite her to join the Committee of Management and she was elected in May at a meeting at Park Crescent.

THIS PLAQUE HAS BEEN ERECTED
IN GRATITUDE TO
MAUREEN
MARCHIONESS OF DUFFERIN
AND AVA
WHO GAVE THE LAND ON WHICH
THE HORDER CENTRE IS BUILT
AND WHO HELPED ALSO
IN MANY OTHER WAYS

The Dufferin Plaque

She proved to be a most generous and energetic benefactor. With her husband she raised large sums of money and her social contacts were exploited to the full. From September 1959 committee meetings took place in her house at 4 Hans Crescent in London SW1. She took collecting boxes around and was a great fund raiser. In March 1960 she organised a royal film premiere for the Centres which raised over £210 000 and she and Judge Maude opened the Owl House Gardens in Lamberhurst to boost funds. In 1960 she purchased the land upon which the Horder Centre was to be built from the War Department and in 1963 gave part of it to the Centre. The plaque recording this was erected in 1970 and the stone plinth on which it was mounted can still be seen at the entrance to the Centre.

Following the unexpected death of Countess Mountbatten, the Marchioness approached Princess Margaret and at a meeting in December 1960 with Judge Maude in the chair it was announced that Her Royal Highness Princess Margaret had graciously accepted the invitation to become their President.

The Owl House Gardens

Maureen, Marchioness of Dufferin and Ava when she started her gardens.

It is not surprising that in due course two such energetic and forceful personalities as the Marchioness and Bochenek would fall out. In 1996, at the age of 89, the Marchioness wrote to the then secretary at the Horder Centre offering the services of Maureen's Oast House for Arthritics, which she owned, as a convalescent centre for patients after joint replacement surgery, a new activity at the Centre of which she strongly approved. In her letter she explained why back in 1966 she had resigned from the committee. She wrote: "But alas eventually I found that what I considered to be in the best interests of the incoming arthritic patients and those of Miss Bochenek were clashing too often. I won't go into it as it would be unfair with Miss Bochenek not being here to put her side. After all, the original marvellous concept had been Miss Bochenek's so I felt for the sake of peace it was best that I very sadly resign from the committee. I feel it only fair though to point out that no less than eight other members of the committee felt as I did and resigned for the same reasons at the same time". She transferred her energy into running Maureen's Oast House for Arthritics in Lamberhurst, a charity which she had founded in 1961, and in 1968 she asked for the words "Maureen Dufferin Place" to be removed from the Horder Centre's letter heading, leaflets and so on.

There can be little doubt, as we shall see, that without the generosity and drive of the Marchioness during her association with the project from 1960 until she resigned in 1966, the Horder Centre would probably not have been built. Although she generously acknowledged in the letter of 1996 that the original concept was that of Bochenek, her own contribution was fundamental to the overall success of the enterprise.

Maureen, Marchioness of Dufferin and Ava died of a stroke in 1998 in London and was buried in Ireland at Clandeboye alongside her first husband Basil and her son Sheridan who pre-deceased her.

Further Reading

1. Edwina, Countess Mountbatten of Burma by Richard Hough. Weidenfeld & Nicholson; 1983. p149

2. ibid p 221.

3. Why not say what happened? A Memoir by Ivana Lowell. Bloomsbury Publishing plc; 2010. p8.

4. Ibid p13.

Establishing the Charity and Early Management Difficulties

In May 1959 discussion took place in committee regarding the appeal for 1959. In reply to a question from Judge Maude as to what was their immediate target, by which he probably had in mind their immediate aim or purpose, Bochenek "explained that our immediate target is the setting up of a residential centre for badly disabled arthritics who will stay for about three months. Most of these patients are likely to be in the age-group eighteen to fifty. The patients we want to help are those who have been told by hospitals that nothing more can be done for them and who are therefore looked upon as permanently unemployable".

THE HORDER CENTRES FOR ARTHRITICS

AIMS

To help arthritic patients of all ages by setting up residential centres of three types :—

Type 1 Centres in which patients are received for a stay of two or three months on the recommendation of a private doctor or hospital. These patients must be so far disabled that they cannot go out to work or carry out normal household duties. Our aim will be to help these people to become once again useful and happy (though still handicapped) members of the community and to lessen the danger of their becoming bed-ridden or chairbound. Experience has shown us that many quite severely affected patients are able to return to their jobs or run their own homes when helped in the right way.

Type 2 Centres for children suffering from Still's disease (a form of juvenile arthritis). These young patients will be given treatment and a first-class education so that when grown-up they are equipped to earn their living in spite of their physical handicaps.

Type 3 Centres for the reception of arthritics who are homeless or who have no-one to care for them.

This appears to be the first detailed statement of the formal aims of the organisation although it may have been incorporated in part in various documents titled *Rules*, which had been written to satisfy the Registrar of Friendly Societies with which the organisation was then registered. The aims were formally defined in the front of the report for 1958. The first annual report was apparently written in 1957 but this has not been found. However, by 1963 these aims had changed somewhat.

The 1958 aims are illustrated. Three types of Centre are described. Type 1 was for those likely to respond to treatment in the Centre, Type 2 was for children with Still's disease and Type 3 was for the homeless or destitute.

However, as matters progressed and the Centre at Crowborough was being built the aims were modified and in 1963 they were redefined. There was still reference to Centres rather than "a Centre". The first Centre was to admit only those with arthritis who were of working age. It was still intended that Centres for elderly and child patients with arthritis would be built later and the concept of home visiting by members of local branches of Horder Centres Helpers were now incorporated into the aims. By now the registered office was at Maureen Dufferin Place, Crowborough where Bochenek and Peake were living in the new bungalow.

Registration of the charity

The Horder Centre was apparently first registered as a charity by Bochenek and presumably Peake in April 1952 with the old London County Council (LCC). They registered the fledgling Society under the *National Assistance Act 1948* later replaced by the *Charities Act 1960*. The name they gave it was "Recuperative Homes for Arthritics" and the original registration details read: "Rules Model H2 (Charitable) published by the National Federation of Housing Societies, Register No: 14132 London. 10th April 1952". This date is almost certainly the original founding date of what was to become the Horder Centre. However, it was not until 1 December 1954 that a notice appeared in the papers using a different name that they had adopted following discussions with Lord Horder.

"Notice is hereby given that it is proposed to apply to the London County Council for the REGISTRATION in accordance with the

National Assistance Act 1948 of "The Horder Centres for Arthritics" the objects of which are shortly as follows: 'To provide residential centres for the treatment and remedial training of persons suffering from Arthritis, and the administrative centre of which is situated at 17 Rugby Mansions, Bishop Kings Road, London W14.' "

The process by which the Centre became registered with the Charity Commissioners proved to be long and arduous. To apply the description used by Churchill in a different context would seem to be reasonable. It was indeed "a riddle, wrapped in a mystery inside an enigma". The committee now met regularly in Bochenek's flat in Bishop Kings Road and in 1956 the treasurer, Mr Webber, warned that the Inland Revenue commissioners did not regard the organisation as a charity. Bochenek contacted the chief inspector of taxes who advised "that we establish our position now". The Registrar of Friendly Societies was approached and told Bochenek that the *Rules* would have to change, which Mr Perkins, a lawyer on the committee, agreed to do without a fee. However, by the next meeting another letter had been received from the tax inspector stating that they agreed after all to regard the Centre as a charity.

In 1961 the Charity Commissioners circulated a document to all interested parties including the Horder Centres. Amongst other details it pointed out that until the *Charities Act 1960* there was no general register of charities in England and Wales. The document outlined the position as it existed now that the new Act was in force, and a follow-up letter in 1962 drew attention to the need for the Horder Centres to register in line with this new Act. "This registration is quite distinct from the registration under the *National Assistance Act* 1948 and the fact that a charity is so registered does not exempt it from registration under the *Charities Act*." Bochenek responded to this by applying to register as a charity under the new Act.

A letter from the Commission in May 1963 confirmed the registration of the Horder Centres for Arthritics and its charity number 211622, with a projected annual income of £350 000. The object of the organisation was recorded as "Providing accommodation, treatment and remedial training for persons suffering from arthritis or kindred diseases". An accompanying letter drew attention to the fact that the commissioners noted the charity had no permanent endowment and they asked for a report on its activities to be sent to them in 5 years' time.

They wrote again in 1967 in response to enquiries by Bochenek seeking to clarify the position then. Although the Centres were registered as a charity, they were constituted as a housing society, which came under the guidance of the Registrar of Friendly Societies. The commissioners stated that they did not wish to become involved with any conflict with the Registrar's field of influence, nor to appear to concern themselves with the organisation or activities of the Centres under their present *Rules*. Soon after this the committee reviewed the situation and it was proposed that the Centres should change their charitable status and become The Horder Centres for Arthritics Charity Trust. However, after a good deal of correspondence had passed between the commissioners and Bochenek, "the committee decided to remain for the time being with the Registrar of Friendly Societies".

Further confusion arose in January 1973 when a letter was received from the commissioners saying that they were under the impression that the Centre had gone ahead with the proposed 1968 scheme and was now registered under the provisions of the *Charities Act 1960* with the number 259454. Bochenek informed them that the change had not been made and the Centres had remained with the Registrar of Friendly Societies. The commissioners replied by saying that they had received no reports from the Charity since 1968 but accepted that the proposal they had put forward then had not gone ahead. Reports were then sent to them by Bochenek.

A great deal more correspondence was generated in 1977 when it was decided to resubmit the application to obtain 'full' charitable status rather than remain with the Registrar of Friendly Societies. Bochenek applied for removal from the Registry on the grounds that the Centres did not provide housing nor distribute benevolent funds and therefore membership requirements as set out by the National Federation of Housing Societies were inappropriate. However this change was not as straightforward as she had hoped. New rules were required by both the Charity Commissioners and the Registrar of Friendly Societies. Letters and telephone calls went back and forth and in due course after new *Rules* had been agreed with the Registrar the status quo was maintained once again. Whether the commissioners accepted the new *Rules* or not is unclear.

A change finally took place much later in 1996. In a letter from the then chief executive of the Centre, John Ball to Lady Dufferin he wrote "You may recall from correspondence in February 1995 the Centre was, yet again, trying to register its charitable function with the Charity Commission and to dissolve the Society from the original governing body, the Registry of Friendly Societies". As part of the process of re-registration of the Centre as a Charitable Company Limited by Guarantee the commissioners wished to know if Lady Dufferin was happy for the land she had donated to be used by the new charitable company. The Marchioness, who was then 89 years old and still living at Hans Crescent, confirmed in her reply that she did consent to the change. On this occasion the change was finally made and the Horder Centre for Arthritis became incorporated under the Companies Acts as a limited company and a registered charity.

Early Management Difficulties

From the time of its foundation until the death of Cecilia Bochenek in 1981 the Centre had seven chairmen overseeing its affairs. Five of these served for relatively short periods. The second, EFJ Perkins Esq., was in office for 7 years and the last, Sir Derek Gilbey, carried on for 9 years at a time when the Centre was struggling to survive.

Chairmen of the Committee of Management 1954 - 1983

Dates in Office	Name		Date of Assuming Office
1954 -1957	Philip Shephard Esq.	1st Chairman	date unknown
1957-1964	E.F.J. Perkins Esq.		4th Jan 1957
1964 – 1966	Sir Edwin Leather M.P.		4th Jun 1964
1966 - 1968	Air Chief Marshal Sir Walter Cheshire GBE., KCB		23rd Mar 1966
1968 - 1970	Richard Medley Esq.		9th Jul 1968
1970 - 1973	Professor RSF Schilling MD FRCP DPH		19th Dec 1970
1974 - 1983	Sir Derek Gilbey, Bart.		27th Apr 1974

Judge Maude's proposals of 1964

On a number of occasions during 1963, Judge Maude had drawn attention to the need for better financial control. The committee had had considerable difficulty in finding a replacement for the treasurer Mr Webber who wished to retire. The Judge considered there was a need for budgeting and had been in contact with a Mr Penfold, the chief accountant at the Middlesex Hospital who was about to retire. Judge Maude hoped that when he had retired Mr Penfold would help with the budget, which it was agreed would need constant review. However, at the next meeting it was decided that the Centre's accountant Mr W.H. Roberts, FCA should be asked if he would attend committee meetings and help with budgeting. It was considered unnecessary, should a finance officer be appointed, to go outside the committee for a treasurer whose duties would then be purely nominal.

Mr Roberts was approached and agreed to be appointed to the post. Terms of reference were drawn up by him and the retiring treasurer, which were accepted by the committee and in November 1963 he was appointed finance officer to the Horder Centres. Sir Hugh Dawson agreed to take over the post of Honorary Treasurer and tributes were paid to Mr Webber for his many years of service on the committee.

Mr Roberts' tenure as finance officer did not last long. In December 1965 he resigned, citing pressure of work elsewhere as the reason. However, the minutes record a statement from him saying that "he did not think it would be fair to give up his position as finance officer without telling the committee that he had always thought that a finance officer should take an active part in all financial affairs, but this had not happened and he had not been invited to participate in important decisions with financial implications of the past twelve months. He thought it right that the committee should evolve a way of changing this state of affairs for his successor". Bochenek responded by taking control of the situation, informing the committee that she had found an accountant, a Mr Hodgens, who had had wide experience as a government finance officer in the Colonial Service and who would be a very suitable replacement. He was retired and living near the Centre. His appointment was apparently approved by the committee without objection, or for that matter an interview.

In addition to advocating more formal financial control as opposed to the rather casual arrangements that had previously been in force, Judge Maude had updated the *Rules of the Centres*. A defining moment came at a meeting which took place in January 1964 at Hans Crescent when a whole series of proposals were put forward by the Judge, supported by various members of the committee, prominent amongst them being Sir Edwin Leather. These proposals sought to put the management of the Centres firmly under the supervision of a broader group of people rather than a sole administrator, to be precise Bochenek. Four sub-committees were set up namely Finance, Branches, Building and Appeals. Detailed guidance on the way they were to be managed was laid down. The chairman of any sub-committee was to be appointed by the Committee of Management and it was agreed that a shorthand typist would be appointed "to attend meetings of the committee to keep the minutes in accordance with the directions of the committee of management as set out in the regulations". All the proposals the Judge put forward were "resolved accordingly" without dissent.

There can be little doubt that the learned Judge, strongly supported by Sir Edwin Leather MP, who was to take over as chairman in June on the retirement of Mr Perkins, had realised that the time for a more formal approach to the running of the organisation had now arrived. Clearly he had come to the conclusion that much greater accountability was needed and that there was little financial control over the significant sums of money that were now being raised from the public and spent on the buildings and expenses. The enthusiasm and commitment of Bochenek and Peake was not in question but the need for proper audit and appraisal was not only required by those who were donating money to the project but was also necessary to satisfy the Charity Commissioners and the tax authorities. The meeting in January 1964 sought to lay down the future management and financial structure of the Centre and to introduce an air of transparency into its affairs, which had previously been hidden or absent.

Further insight into the problems that had concerned Judge Maude can be found in a letter he wrote to Bochenek shortly after he put his proposals to the committee. In the letter dated 21 February 1964 he thanked Bochenek and Peake for their kindness after he had visited Crowborough to discuss the matter of the proposed *Rules for Branches* and then using his very considerable diplomatic skills he raised another matter on which he had given further thought. Extracts from his letter are as follows:

"I am referring to my having said that I would propose you for the Committee of Management. I have now given this question very careful consideration and I have come to the conclusion that I should <u>not</u> do this; ... I have come to the conclusion that so much of the money which is received from the public has to be spent on your own salary and other expenses that it would not be right for you to be a member of the Committee of Management. ... The drain upon the resources of the Society which we are facing with the impending further expenditure upon building is extremely formidable and I consider that your own position as an employee of the Society who receives a very considerable salary [her salary had been agreed at today's equivalent of £24,000 per annum in October 1962] would make your position on the Committee one of very great difficulty. I can see many matters upon which the Committee would have to decide regarding expenditure which might well conflict with your own views as to how money should be spent, particularly when funds are so strained. ... I do think however that you should not as a paid officer of the Society, in present circumstances, be in a position which might lay the Society open to considerable criticism."

Dr Peake in Bungalow Garden

This letter clearly touched a raw nerve with Peake, who wrote in the margin "she brings money in. CB has saved HCA thousands!" She and Bochenek, however, were now living rent free with free heating and lighting in the new purpose-built bungalow in Crowborough, which they had moved into in December 1962 and she was working on the garden. The need to avoid giving the impression, even if quite unjustified, that they were perhaps benefiting unduly from the fruits of their labours clearly was not appreciated by her.

Unfortunately, Judge Maude became seriously ill in April 1964 and although at one time it was hoped that he would return to the committee, in February 1965 he tendered his resignation on health grounds. The management changes he had proposed, and which had been agreed by the Committee of Management in January 1964, were not therefore guided through in the way they might have been had he been active on the committee during that year. Had the committee followed Judge Maude's lucid and wise guidance as they should have done, some of the problems which occurred later might have been avoided. Sir Edwin Leather, in a long letter to Bochenek following a meeting with her and Peake when he took over as chairman in June 1964, did his best to smooth ruffled feathers with "I so hope that with a determined effort from all of us concerned we are going to get this committee going ahead again amicably and efficiently". He identified quite correctly that many of the recent disagreements had arisen because of the relationship between the Centre and the Helpers. He did his best to introduce changes and indeed improved accountability did come about during his term of office. However, after what might have been called in a later era a 'hand bagging', as recorded in the nine pages of minutes of a committee meeting held in February 1966, he decided that his duties as a Member of Parliament required his full attention and he retired to the relative calm of the House of Commons. It was left to the incoming chairman, Air Chief Marshal Sir Walter Cheshire to restore good order and military discipline at the next meeting a month later.

A Royal President
and Fund Raising

The business plan, if it can be referred to as such, upon which the early financial arrangements were based was simple. In essence it involved persuading those who are sometimes called the 'Great and the Good' to dig deep into their pockets to provide the capital and income on which the project depended for its growth. Great efforts were also made to attract smaller donations from the general public. Expenses were kept to a minimum and whenever possible people were asked to donate their services freely. Neither Bochenek nor Peake were wealthy and what income they had in the early days seems to have come from Bochenek's teaching at Rugby

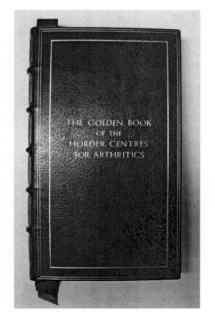

Mansions and a limited amount of private medical practice that Peake carried on at the same address.

This plan succeeded in the early days due to Bochenek's powers of persuasion and with the assistance of one or two key figures considerable capital sums were raised. However, the cost of the building development was such that the opportunity to build up a significant endowment to provide an income stream in the future when running costs would became larger was denied them. In the report given at the Annual General Meeting (AGM) in March 1960, it was reported that it was hoped that 1961 would see the first stage of building under way. "At first it will be possible to admit relatively few arthritics, owing to the huge cost of building. How soon we are able to finish the complete Centre to accommodate 100 arthritics and the necessary staff depends entirely on how quickly the money comes in." As capital flowed in so it went out, spent on the building development and as activity increased, to offset expenditure on salaries and running costs. This as will be seen led to difficulties once the Centre had opened when it became increasingly difficult to obtain adequate funding for patients from the various statutory authorities.

One of Bochenek's great talents bolstered by her innate enthusiasm and determination was her willingness to approach anyone be they the highest or lowest in the land if she thought they would help. One of her more novel ideas for raising funds was the *Golden Book*. When she introduced this idea to Lady Mountbatten in 1956 shortly after she succeeded Lord Horder as President, the Countess gave it her full support.

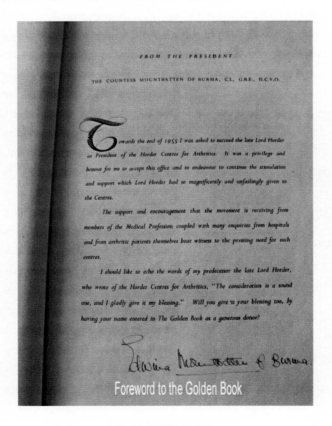

Foreword to the Golden Book

38

At the meeting in February 1956, at which the chairman Philip Shephard announced that Countess Mountbatten of Burma had graciously accepted the office of President, Bochenek explained her idea to the committee. In the book "would be written the names of firms and individuals giving, say, five pounds or more. This book should be rather imposing and very well bound, and should be on view at the Registered Office and later in the first Centre". She had discussed this with Lady Mountbatten who was willing to write a few words appealing for funds on the first page and she intended also to ask the vice-presidents to sign a page indicating support.

In due course an agreement was reached with two firms: Messrs Franey & Co., who would produce the book and illuminate Lady Mountbatten's message and other pages and Messrs Sangorski & Sutcliffe, who would bind it. Both firms generously offered to produce the book free of charge. It was finally presented to the committee for examination in October. All were greatly impressed by the excellent workmanship and Bochenek was asked to write again to the two firms expressing the appreciation of the committee. A few of the more notable entries are given below. The size of some donations is striking, particularly those given by the Marchioness of Dufferin and Ava.

Much discussion took place as to when and how the launch date should be arranged. Eventually the occasion was staged at Selfridges in Oxford Street in March 1957 in co-operation with the Columbia Gramophone Company during the "Ruby Murray 'Heart' Week". Bochenek and Peake spent the week at the store and the book was apparently exhibited in the main window. Ruby Murray was a popular singer at the time who had recently released a recording of her song "Heart". She had generously offered the royalties from this recording to the Centre and in due course the sum of £6200 was received. She was the first contributor to sign her name in the *Golden Book* on a special "Stars Page". Winifred Attwell was the other.

The first of the main entries start on the next page, headed by Countess Mountbatten who donated £630. Many famous people contributed including Her Excellency Mrs Lakshmi Pandit, Nehru's sister and The High Commissioner for India, who was one of Edwina's greatest admirers. In 1961 Bochenek was able to record with pride "It is with the greatest satisfaction and gratitude that we record that Her Majesty the Queen has been graciously pleased to make a grant towards the cost of building the first

Centre". In addition in November 1967, to celebrate the first anniversary of the Centre, Bochenek informed the committee that Her Majesty had graciously agreed that a grant would be made from the Privy Purse on 1 November each year and Her Majesty has been graciously pleased to allow this to continue to the present day. The *Golden Book* is preserved at the Centre and provides a useful insight into the degree and source of support that its two creators achieved when they established it.

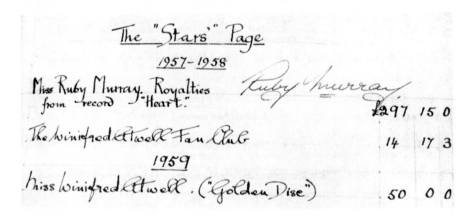

From 1959 onwards several entries recording donations from the Marchioness Dufferin and Ava are found. She gave by covenant £490 monthly and £570 annually. Her husband Judge John Maude QC was also a generous contributor. In 1961 a donation of £23 000 from Lady Dufferin is noted following the opening of her Owl House Garden at Lamberhurst. However the individual donation record lapses after 1965, the last entry being one made after the Marchioness had staged an All Star Variety show in London which raised £64 000. After that date the *Golden Book* was used to record the dates of important events in the history of the Centre. Foremost amongst these are the times when HRH Princess Margaret visited the Centre to open new departments or extensions. On all these occasions the Princess signed the *Golden Book*, her last recorded visit being on the 27 October 2000 when she opened the newly re-furbished out-patient department.

When the Marchioness joined the committee in May 1959 the funds stood at £77 000. Recent fund-raising activities had involved approaches to various Trusts and publicity in newspapers, both national and local, often through the medium of the Horder Centres Helpers, which were being set up around the country. This had resulted in a number of relatively modest donations being received but administrative costs were inevitably beginning to rise. An attempt had been made by advertising in *The Times* and *The Daily Telegraph* to obtain a house, presumably through a legacy, which would have provided more office space. Only a few enquiries were received.

The arrival of the Marchioness was about to change all that. In 1955 and again in 1956 attempts had been made to set up an appeals committee but little seems to have come from these proposals. The meetings of the committee had been held for the past year in the waiting room of a GP, Dr Laws, in 13 Park Crescent W1 but as she was about to retire another room was needed. The Marchioness "very kindly offered to have the meetings in her private residence. Her ladyship's kind offer was accepted with deep gratitude". She also offered to pay the rent of a second room at 17 Rugby Mansions, which was needed as office accommodation. The first meeting at her house, 4 Hans Crescent, Knightsbridge took place in September 1959.

The Marchioness began to influence the fund-raising activity to an increasing degree. A fashion show at her house had raised £800 for the Centres. At the October meeting she was elected appeals chairman. She also became chairman of the Horder Centres Helpers. By the end of the year funds had increased from £70 000 in January to £150 000. Several new Helpers Branches had been set up including The Lady Dufferin Branch with the Marchioness as chairman. In December she announced that she had been successful in obtaining the premiere of the film "Once More with Feeling", which would

HRH Princess Margaret with the Marchioness of Dufferin and Ava meet Cecilia Bochenek and Dr Peake at a fund-raising event.

take place at the Scala Theatre and that HRH Princess Margaret and Lord Snowdon had promised to attend. This appears to be the first mention of the involvement of the Princess with the Centre. The event took place in March 1960 and raised over £190 000 for the funds.

Following the successful film first night, which took place shortly after the death of Countess Mountbatten, the Marchioness approached Princess Margaret and asked her to become President of the Centres and at the committee meeting on 15 December 1960 it was announced that HRH Princess Margaret, Countess of Snowdon had graciously accepted an invitation to be President of the Horder Centres. Again "A very hearty vote of thanks to Lady Dufferin was carried with acclamation". In June 1960 she opened her gardens at Lamberhurst and raised £7000, a function which she repeated in the following year.

HRH Princess Margaret, Countess of Snowdon,
Third President of the Horder Centres

When the Princess agreed to become President of the Centres following the sudden death of Edwina, Countess Mountbatten of Burma there may well have been some who thought that the appointment was merely a symbolic one and that apart from an occasional formal visit it would be unlikely, in view of her many royal commitments, that Her Royal Highness would find time to play a very active role in the affairs of the Centre. They could not have been more mistaken.

In 1963 she presided at the AGM at the Royal Commonwealth Society in London and would have done so again in 1964 had she not just given birth to her daughter. She was present again in 1965 and 1966, on these occasions at the Royal Society of Medicine, and in October of that same year she opened the new Centre at Crowborough. During the period of fund raising in the run up to the opening she attended a number of major fund-raising events in London that had been organised by the Marchioness. After the AGM in 1968, which she attended, the meetings appear to have been held on a biennial basis and she attended these in 1971 and 1973. She made private visits to Crowborough to assess progress in 1968, 1975 and again in 1978 and on this last occasion on her return to London instructed her solicitors to provide advice regarding difficulties the Committee was having with building contractors. She visited on several occasions in the 1980s and 1990s to open new facilities and when she opened the first operating theatre in 1990 she made a personal call on Dr Joyce Peake in her private quarters a few weeks before Joyce Peake died. Her twelfth and last visit was on 27 October 2000 when she opened the re-furbished out-patient department. Her close and abiding interest in the development and progress of the Horder Centre during the 42 years in which she was its President provided a constant source of inspiration to all who worked or were treated there.

Another great achievement of the Marchioness was her purchase in 1960 of the site on which the first Centre was to be built. At a meeting in July at Hans Crescent, she announced that she wished to instruct her agent to secure a site in Crowborough. The committee agreed that if necessary there should be a contribution from the funds of the Centres and the following resolution was passed: "This committee welcomes the news that Lady Dufferin will purchase the site, and agrees, if necessary, to make the sum of £12,000 (£230,000) available towards the purchase". In September however it was noted that the land had already been purchased and the Marchioness had not taken up the offer from the committee, having paid for it herself at a cost today of £310 000. "A very hearty vote of thanks proposed from the chair was carried unanimously and with great acclamation" when it was recorded that the site had been purchased and shortly afterwards, Crabtree & Associates were appointed architects to the Centres.

At the time of the AGM in March 1962, held at the Royal Commonwealth Society, Princess Margaret was unwell and therefore unable to attend as she had intended. However she sent a message which was read out by the chairman in which she expressed the gratitude of everyone "to Lady Dufferin, the Appeals Chairman, for her generosity in donating the wonderful site at Crowborough for the new Centre". By now there was £470 000 available in the funds and this together with the gift of land enabled planning to take place for building to start in 1962.

In 1961 and 1962 the Marchioness opened her Owl House Garden at Lamberhurst, raising over £23 000 on both occasions and she organised a Gala First Night performance of "Vanity Fair", which was attended by Princess Margaret and Lord Snowdon in November 1962. In 1963, a charity party was held at Crockford's on behalf of the Centres and another charity, which raised £16 000 for the Centres, the Marchioness acting as hostess. An exhibition at Cartier's in Bond Street also attended by Princess Margaret and Lord Snowdon was a great financial success. By now Bochenek and Peake were living in the bungalow at Crowborough, this building and the administrative block having opened at the end of 1962. In September 1963 a big fête was organised at Crowborough, the organising committee for this event being chaired by Lady De La Warr. She was assisted by the Marchioness who apparently arranged for the ex-army tank sheds adjacent to the Centre's site to be used to save the expense of hiring a marquee. The remains of these tank sheds still stand today and fall just outside the parcel of land that was donated to the Centres by the Marchioness.

Throughout the year, Bochenek and Peake, with a small staff of typists, worked tirelessly to publicise these activities and raise the profile of the Centres in the eyes of the public. The fête went a long way to raise awareness in the community at Crowborough about the purpose of the proposed new buildings and helped to allay the fears of those locally who regarded this new development in their midst with some apprehension. Numerous local agencies, such as the Red Cross, the Women's Voluntary Services, the Boy Scouts and Girl Guides, the Appeals Committee of Crowborough Hospital, the tennis club, the police, Southdown Motor Services, who put on extra buses and countless individuals were all approached and willingly lent their services. The fête was clearly a major occasion and raised over £36 000. The function became a regular public awareness and fund-raising event and was later called the "Rainbow Fair" usually taking place at the Centre in September or October.

The 1963 AGM had taken place on 19 March in the Assembly Hall of the Royal Commonwealth Society in the presence of Princess Margaret. After the chairman Mr Perkins had invited the Princess to address the meeting, Her Royal Highness described how the bungalow and office accommodation had already been built and the site prepared for the main block. Twenty eight branches of Horder Centres Helpers had been established and "Our thanks go to those people who give their time to assist and comfort others and in raising funds for the organization". Lady Dufferin and Bochenek also spoke, followed by Sir Edwin Leather, the then chairman of the Bristol branch of Helpers, on behalf of the Helpers.

In April 1963 the first rift in the relationship between The Marchioness and Bochenek occurred. This concerned the running of the London branches of Helpers and during the ensuing discussions both Bochenek and Peake threatened to resign. Eventually matters were temporarily resolved but further problems would soon arise. In May of that year Bochenek, now calling herself the administrator, reported that Lord Dufferin, the Marchioness's son Sheridan, had very kindly signed a 7-year covenant for £9000 per annum. However at a meeting shortly afterwards, Judge Maude explained that his Lordship's financial advisors, not realising that the covenant was for a charity, had given him the wrong figures and the annual sum would produce about £2600 for the Centre. The original covenant was returned to Lord Dufferin for cancellation.

The AGM in 1964 seems to have been a low key event if it took place at all. It was planned to occur in May at County Hall Westminster but no record of the proceedings has been found. That year saw two major fund-raising events. In September 1964, as in the previous year, the

Centre put on its "Rainbow Fair" again. Unfortunately the date clashed with the Crowborough Carnival although a number of people apparently attended both events and a net profit of just under £26 000 was made. The Crowborough Bonfire Society kindly decided to divide the profits from their carnival between the Friends of Crowborough Hospitals and the Horder Centre and invited Bochenek and Peake to their annual dinner to receive the cheque for £850. In November the Marchioness (chairman of the executive committee for the variety show) and Primrose, Countess Cadogan (vice-chairman) organised a variety show to raise funds at the Scala Theatre in London, which was attended by Princess Margaret and Lord Snowdon. The show raised £62 000 for the Centre. The Marchioness again opened the Owl House Garden during the year.

In September it was reported that "the committee felt that it should not continue to take advantage of Lady Dufferin's kindness which for some time had enabled them to hold meetings at her London house". From September 1964 according to the annual report for that year and after the matter had been discussed with Lady Dufferin, all future meetings were held in the welfare department of the London County Council at 10 Warwick Road SW1, free of charge.

The AGM in 1965 was held in March in the presence of HRH Princess Margaret. Lord Cohen, President of the Royal Society of Medicine, gave permission for the large hall of the Society in Wimpole Street to be used for the meeting and he also made the President's Room available so that the Princess could be invited to tea afterwards. Bochenek arranged floral decorations and for a young girl with arthritis to present flowers to the Princess.

In the course of that year, development of the central block and first patient accommodation reached the stage where decoration and furnishing needed to be discussed. A meeting of the house sub-committee took place in October. It was chaired by Sir Edwin Leather and attended by the Marchioness and her advisor, together with Lady Cadogan, Lady Leather and the architect Mr Senkowsky as well as Bochenek and Peake. It was decided that the interior decorations and furnishings of the medical treatment and consulting rooms would be the responsibility of Bochenek and Peake. The interior decoration of all other rooms and the passages were to be the sole responsibility of Lady Dufferin and her interior design advisor Miss Peggy Hancock. Discussions on furnishings, curtains, carpets and paint colours then followed. Wallpaper for the rooms and staircases were to be chosen by the Marchioness always with the proviso that cost should be kept low if possible. This meeting seems to have achieved, with difficulty, agreement on the way forward but at the next meeting in January discord resurfaced. From then on the relationship between the Marchioness with others from the Lady Dufferin Branch of Helpers and Bochenek and Peake deteriorated. At the committee meeting in February 1966 Sir Edwin announced Lady Dufferin's resignation as appeals chairman. The meeting then continued with a general air of dissension amongst the members, finally ending with a discussion on the matter of the annual report. Sir Edwin said that most of the branch reports had been received but there was a problem with the one from the Lady Dufferin Branch. On the balance sheet Lady Dufferin had sent in she was claiming back for her Oast House 25 percent of the money she had recently sent to the Horder Centre after the variety show. This, the Chairman stated "would cause problems for the auditor". At this point the Marchioness retorted "I am claiming more than that now, I am claiming fifty percent". Dr Peake then interjected that in the Lady Dufferin Branch report the proceeds of the All Star Variety Show were reported to be from a branch function rather than from the Centre as a whole. This function she said had been fully reported in the 1964 annual report although the money had not been received. Lady Dufferin then "scratched out the entry and initialled it".

Matters then seem to have gone from bad to worse. In May 1966, with Sir Walter Cheshire now in the chair, Peake's salary was set at £24 000 per annum and her title as Resident Medical Director was confirmed. At the next meeting in July the Marchioness referred to this matter stating that she, Lady Cadogan and Mr Neelands had asked to go on record as having voted against this motion. However the minutes secretary later confirmed, following a request from the chairman, that she had no record of this, although she had been asked to record that they had voted against the motion voted on just before the one on Dr Peake's salary, which was concerned with setting a date for the opening of the Centre. Mr Perkins who had been present had abstained on this. The chairman had apparently announced that HRH Princess Margaret would open the Centre formally on the afternoon of 27 October 1966.

In September the Marchioness and Lady Cadogan said they would not be able to attend the opening on that date. The resignations of Primrose, Countess Cadogan, Mrs GM McNeill-Moss and Mrs Gisle, all from the Lady Dufferin Branch in London, were also announced at that time. The final straw came at the end of this meeting when Dr Sharpe, a friend of Peake who had recently joined the committee, referred to a letter sent on 5 August by the Marchioness, addressed to Peake but circulated to other members of the committee, in which the following sentence appeared: "It is a very long time ago now since you practised, and since poor Miss Bochenek was in hospital you had been doing such a wonderful, all absorbing job raising money for the Horder that it is more than understandable that you had got a little out of touch as to what the great Hospitals after careful thought, have found both practicable and pleasant for the patients". In the ensuing discussion Dr Sharpe said she thought this was an extremely rude and possibly defamatory remark. The Marchioness then said Dr Peake had not been in practice for 13 years, to which Peake replied that she had carried on private practice in Rugby Mansions up to the time she and Miss Bochenek left London. She added, perhaps somewhat surprisingly, that she had not been raising funds. She had sent the letter to the Medical Defence Union who agreed, she informed the committee, that it was defamatory. Mr Perkins, perhaps seeking to pour a little oil on the turbulent waters, expressed his opinion that the letter sprang from a genuine desire to do the best for the Horder Centre but others thought it was regrettable that it had been circulated.

Although the Marchioness had perhaps been wrong to send this letter to other members of the committee the main tenet of her argument was reasonable. Peake was now 64, well past the age of retirement for a female medical practitioner in those days and it was undoubtedly true that she had not been in mainstream practice for many years. The Marchioness may well have thought, quite reasonably, that a younger person with more up-to-date ideas would be more suitable for the post of Medical Director. How in practice such an appointment could ever have been orchestrated is hard to imagine.

At the following meeting on 23 November 1966 just after the opening of the Centre by Princess Margaret, Sir Walter Cheshire told the committee that Lady Dufferin had resigned shortly after the last meeting. This rather sad end to the association between the Marchioness and the Centre, which had started when she used her considerable influence to involve her distinguished and wealthy friends in its development, thus raising the profile of the Centre when it was virtually unknown, meant that the way forward was now going to be much more difficult. Thus were sown the seeds of many problems that troubled the Centre throughout the seventies and which by the early eighties very nearly led to its closure.

THE HORDER CENTRES HELPERS

Horder Centres Helpers were first mentioned in the minutes of the Committee of Management in October 1956. After Bochenek had written a number of letters to the press, some small donations had been received and "an arthritic had formed a group of Horder Centres Helpers. They are working to augment our funds and are distributing leaflets". After some discussion it was agreed that these people had shown initiative and goodwill and there was no objection to them opening a bank account in their name as they had asked, from which "they will deduct expenses and send us the profits".

This seems to have been the beginning of the Horder Centres Helpers. In February 1957 a meeting of the Executive Committee took place, although this title, an unintentional substitution perhaps for Bochenek and Peake, had never been mentioned before, to meet a Miss Pamment. She had called to discuss the formation of the first branch of the Horder Centres Helpers at Thorpe near Norwich.

After this discussion Bochenek informed the committee that she had been in touch with the London County Council (LCC) and had been told that as soon as the committee gave written permission for Miss Pamment's group to call themselves "Horder Centres Helpers" this group would become automatically affiliated to the Horder Centres for Arthritics. A contract was drawn up in which it was clearly stated that "the aim of the Helpers is solely to raise funds for the Horder Centres". Miss Pamment was thanked and asked to convey the best wishes of the committee to her group.

The founding of the Helpers clearly arose as a result of this initiative by Miss Pamment in Norwich. Unfortunately this Branch did not survive for long and had closed by 1960, and the first regular branch to be set up was later stated by Bochenek to be that at Sutton and Cheam in 1957. However Bochenek was quick to realise the potential the idea presented and the aims were soon widened to include visits to people with arthritis in their homes as well as fund raising. A letter in *The Daily Telegraph* led to considerable interest and in the 1958 annual report Bochenek was able to state that there were now five branches that were "affiliated to the Horder Centres for Arthritics".

In November 1959 the Lady Dufferin branch was registered with the LCC under the chairmanship of Lady Dufferin who had also agreed to be chairman of the Horder Centres Helpers as a whole. By now there were 16 branches with 670 Helpers looking after 420 arthritics. During the period 1961-1964 the Helpers contributed over £240 000 to the funds of the Centres.

In the 1959 annual report their function was described in some detail and this was repeated in subsequent reports. It was explained that branches were affiliated to the Horder Centres for Arthritics and were thus registered with the LCC. The LCC required written permission from the Centre to be given for any activities such as lotteries, draws and pools. An annual report including a financial statement had to be sent to the administrator (Bochenek). The Branch could keep 25 percent of the money it raised for expenses with the remaining 75 percent to be sent to the Centres. Their most valuable work was "in befriending home-bound arthritics who are lonely and depressed. Their visits are friendly and informal and are greatly appreciated". They assisted in such tasks as shopping, changing library books and writing letters but no-one was visited without their consent. To safeguard against unauthorised callers posing as Helpers every person who asked to be visited was sent a free life membership card and was told that the caller would show a similar card at the first visit. Both arthritics and Helpers were insured against claims arising from accusations of negligence during visits, or when the patient was being taken out in a wheelchair. The patient was not charged for this insurance, it being "part of the annual subscription of five shillings (£4.80 in 2012) which all Helpers are invited to pay, except in cases where payment would involve difficulty or hardship".

An example of one of the larger branches was that founded in 1960 in Bristol by a Mrs Gwen Balchin. The branch President, Sir Edwin Leather MP later became chairman of the Management Committee of the Centres. A local Councillor Edwin Roberts was chairman and L. Balchin Esq., honorary secretary, with his wife as one of three liaison officers. They organised car outings and day trips though Somerset stopping for entertainment and tea during the trip. A local primary school sang carols for the patients and they set up coffee mornings, car treasure hunts and a "Grand Autumn Faire". In 1960 they raised £12 000 for the funds. Sadly Gwen Balchin died at the young age of 39. The members of the branch asked the Centre if they could plant a tree in her memory at the Centre and on the 26 October 1968 a ceremony was held which was attended by 20 members of the Bristol Branch. This memorial tree, a mountain ash, or *Sorbus* and the dedication plaque are still there near the Dufferin entrance to the Centre. In 2010 a 50-year time capsule was buried alongside this tree with its own plaque.

A curious episode arose shortly after the ceremony. The plaque was

stolen but before its replacement was arranged it was found sticking out of a bush in the grounds of the Centre and was rescued. Clearly the thief's conscience was troubled by his selfish act, a sentiment that seems to be of little concern to the metal thieves of the early twenty-first century.

Good as the branches were, their organisation and running soon led to significant difficulties. Activity at the Blackpool branch gave rise to very unwelcome publicity when *The Sunday People* reported that the secretary had a conviction for fraud. The chairman then disappeared and none of the money collected in the name of the Horder Centres appears to have been received by the Centre. Links with the branch were quickly severed.

In April 1963 the record of a meeting at Hans Crescent provides evidence of an early disagreement between the Marchioness and Bochenek and Peake. The minute was later crossed out but is still easily read. It concerned setting up branches of Helpers in the London area and the appointment of someone to look after these branches overall as advocated by the Marchioness

and Judge Maude. Their concept was that in time this arrangement could be extended to other parts of the country and they had suggested that a Mrs Brocklebank, the organiser of the Lady Dufferin branch, should be appointed to the task.

Mrs Brocklebank, a lady of resolute disposition, apparently did not like having to refer to headquarters. Bochenek maintained that "branches did not need supervising except by headquarters and this control could be exercised just as easily from Crowborough as from London". She realised quite reasonably that without central control matters of registration and insurance together with the requirements of the LCC would be difficult to monitor. She stressed that accurate lists should be sent to headquarters from any branch run by Mrs Brocklebank and that membership cards should be issued only from headquarters. After some discussion it was agreed that these cards should only be issued from head office at Crowborough.

Further discussion followed. "Dr Peake agreed with everything Miss Bochenek had said and added that she did not agree with sending representatives over the country trying to set up branches." Sir Edwin Leather, then President of the Bristol Branch of Helpers, disagreed and said that branches were not being formed nearly fast enough. The chairman, Mr Perkins, resolved matters by setting up a sub-committee to be called "The Horder Centres Helpers Branches Sub-committee" to be chaired by Lady Dufferin, with Mrs McNeill-Moss, Mr Ford, Sir Edwin Leather and Judge Maude as members with powers to co-opt.

Correspondence then ensued between Bochenek and the chairman of the Committee of Management and in a letter in May 1963 Bochenek threatened to resign. She referred to the recently formed branches sub-committee as self-elected and confirmed her belief that the ultimate aim of that group was to alter the working agreement under which the branches had previously been governed, which she had drawn up, so that the London branches were independent of headquarters. She went on to complain about the activities of Lady Dufferin, Mrs Brocklebank and others on the Committee of Management continuing "I was hardly allowed to speak at the meeting, in fact, without flat contradiction. Of course it was obvious to Dr Peake and myself that this procedure had been carefully worked out in advance, as the members knew that Dr Peake and I would not agree with their ideas for taking the running of the branches out of my hands". Finally she stated her intention to give 3 months' notice of her resignation at the next meeting to take effect from the 30 June 1963, although she was careful to qualify it with "unless I have the firm assurance that in future all committee business will be conducted in a completely straightforward way".

A second letter to the chairman was written by Peake on the same date. She reiterated her view that she was in entire agreement with everything Bochenek had written. She added that if Bochenek tendered her resignation she would do the same, although she hoped this would not be necessary and then went on to complain somewhat illogically that "It is a great pity that not one member of the committee appreciated the value of Miss Bochenek's ideas from the medical point of view". As the matter under discussion was an administrative one and not medical it is difficult to see what Bochenek's views on medical matters had to do with it. The sub-committee set up by the chairman to deal with this matter reported to the next meeting on 27 May and differences seem to have been resolved for the time being. It was assumed that for now the London branches would continue to run on the same lines as the other branches.

This battle of wills between Bochenek and Peake on the one hand and the Committee of Management on the other did not bode well for the future. The powerful group of individuals on the committee who mainly resided in Belgravia and Kensington and who had been responsible for raising significant funds in the London area clearly resented any form of control from headquarters which in effect meant Bochenek and Peake. They likewise saw the activities of the London group as an attempt to take over the running of the organisation that they had created and as is seen in surviving records from that time, were understandably upset. Indeed the Marchioness magnanimously recognised this in a letter many years later in 1995 in which she described why she eventually left the committee. She wrote: "After all the original marvellous concept had been Miss Bochenek's so I felt for the sake of peace it was best that I very sadly resign from the Committee" (see Chapter 2). However the eventual loss of these influential supporters weakened the authority of the organisation at the time and made it more difficult to raise money in the future.

In January 1964 Judge Maude introduced proposals aimed at putting the administration on a more accountable footing. With regard to the Helpers specifically it was proposed and adopted that a branches sub-committee would be set up. He advised that a London Liaison Office be formed, its affairs to be conducted by a member or co-opted member of the Committee of Management, to liaise with all the branches of the Society whose postal address was within the London postal district. The Liaison Office was to appear in the telephone directory under the title of Horder Centres Helpers, London Liaison Office. It would have significant autonomous powers although it was required to submit an annual report on activity and finances to head office. After discussion, during which Bochenek drew the attention of the committee to certain difficulties that would arise from the point of view of headquarters, it was resolved that "Judge Maude should accompany Mrs. Brocklebank to headquarters in order to discuss and endeavour to find a way of overcoming all the difficulties which would emanate from these resolutions being put into effect". It was also agreed that setting up this London Liaison Office would be experimental and the experiment would continue for two years from its start.

Shortly after this Mrs Brocklebank was co-opted onto the committee. However Judge Maude had retired due to illness and in July the new chairman, Sir Edwin Leather, having first suggested that all existing sub-committees be dissolved forthwith, a suggestion which was enthusiastically agreed to by some, proposed that he as chairman, the administrator and the medical adviser would draw up new *Rules for the Branches* of the Horder Centres Helpers, which would be presented to the committee and then to a conference of branches to be called in the autumn. In a handwritten letter that he sent to Bochenek from Canada whilst on holiday in August 1964, he wrote that the rules for the Helpers would be basically those drawn up by Judge Maude but with some changes. The most important of these was that "the Helpers should be formally constituted as had been originally intended, that is as an affiliated body and <u>not</u> as an integral part of the Society itself." This was agreed and arrangements were made for the meeting to take place in November at 10 Warwick Row where the committee then met.

This first conference of the branches took place on the 6 November 1964 as planned, and according to Sir Edwin was a very successful and enthusiastic one. The main object had been to consider the newly proposed rules, which were, with certain minor amendments, accepted. This meeting seems to have been the first of what became an annual event that was repeated until 1979. However, somewhat ominously, it was also reported by Sir Edwin that Mrs Brocklebank had sent her resignation to him after the meeting. Mrs McNeill-Moss and others paid tribute to the very hard work she had done as London Liaison Officer.

From then on the relationship between several members of the committee and Bochenek and Peake deteriorated quickly. In February 1966 Lady Dufferin resigned as Appeals Chairman. In July the London Liaison Office was closed following an unsuccessful proposal by Mr Neelands that it should be kept open. His proposal was rejected on a show of hands. That meeting ended with a request from the chairman, now Sir Walter Cheshire, to Lady Dufferin, probably acting on a request from Bochenek, asking her to avoid making appeals to trusts and companies, to which she agreed. In September it was announced that the Lady Dufferin branch of Helpers had returned all its records to the Centre and closed down.

After the opening of the Centre at Crowborough in 1966 the number of branches slowly declined. In 1974 John Taylor from the Bristol branch, who had been co-opted onto the committee as branch representative, drew attention to disquiet that was being expressed by a number of local representatives. The Croydon branch was to be dissolved "in view of great difficulties experienced in dealing with headquarters and the evidence of failing interest locally". Mr Taylor said that he could quite understand the feelings of the Croydon branch members and felt there was a lack of enthusiasm amongst the branches generally and disenchantment with the Centre. Mr Taylor was asked to write to all the branches asking for specific complaints and then to make a summary and pass it to Bochenek to inform management. At the Annual Meeting of the Helpers in June 1975 it was decided that there would no longer be a branch representative on the committee and Peake thought that it would be better to revert to the old system of having direct contact between the branches and the Centre. Mr Taylor said that however it was done contact between the Centre and branches and between the branches themselves was essential. He was concerned "that the number of branches had diminished so much and he felt that unless action was taken now there would be no branches at all in a few years". At the same meeting he announced his retirement as he was moving to Wiltshire and little attention appears to have been paid to his concerns. By December 1975 only seven branches were still functioning and several had closed during the year. At the 15th combined meeting in

1979 only two branches were represented and this appears to have been the last combined meeting.

The branches of Helpers had in effect been a substitute for the other residential centres, which at the time of the foundation it had been envisaged would be built elsewhere in the country, something which never came about. Over the 22 years of their existence branches opened and closed and it is difficult to estimate the number that functioned at any one time. In 1961 Bochenek in a letter appealing for funds referred to over "2000 homebound arthritics being regularly visited by our voluntary Helpers" and in September of that year there were 23 branches. In the annual report of 1964, branch reports from 32 branches were included and this was probably the peak of their existence. Initially they did a great deal to spread the word about the aims of the Centre and raised considerable funds to help with the early building. As time passed and it became clear that the aspiration of building many Centres was unrealistic, the organisers of the various branches gradually lost their enthusiasm and slowly faded from the scene as other national agencies took over their role. They had however provided a great deal of financial and practical support in the early years and had brought comfort to many severely disabled patients who would otherwise have been left to manage their disabilities alone. They had played a major role in the early development of the Horder project.

BUILDING AND STAFFING

I t is not clear why Crowborough was chosen by the Marchioness when she bought the land on which the Centre was to be built but it is likely that she received advice from her agents that the site had become available and was suitable. In 1952 when she bought the Owl House, the oldest building in Kent, situated near Lamberhurst, as a country retreat, she would have got to know the area quite well. In 1960 she bought land as shown in the original Deed of Gift, from the Secretary of State for War. This land had previously been occupied by the military and was known as the Crowborough West Camp. When she bought the site it extended over 54 acres and in March 1963 she gave 12 1/2 acres of this area to the Centre. According to the annual report in 1960 the Marchioness had agreed to give as much of this land as was needed to build the first of the residential Centres.

The old plan, on which the Centre's site is outlined, shows the position of the original camp buildings. The small building seen at the bottom right was the Camp Medical Centre and is in precisely the position now occupied by the bungalow Panorama. The footprint of this building is very similar to that of the bungalow and it seems very likely that in 1962 the old Medical Centre was either demolished or adapted to make way for the bungalow, which was then built on the same foundations.

The Crowborough West Camp was established on the site of an earlier Canadian army camp dating from the

First World War. During the Second World War it was occupied in the early years by the 23rd Armoured Brigade, comprising the 40th, 46th and 50th Royal Tank Regiments who left for the Western Desert in 1942 to be replaced by the Canadian Grenadiers of the 22 Canadian Armoured Regiment. In 1944 the Canadians took part in the fierce fighting in Normandy around Caen and Falaise and then went on into Germany. Very sadly many of these men did not return.

Matilda & Valentine Tanks Crowborough 1942

The Tank Sheds in 2011

After the war the West Camp was occupied by part of the 3rd Infantry Brigade and Peter Deere who worked at the Centre from 1998 until 2005 recalls that in the 1950s his father, CQMS Deere of the Royal Army Service Corps, had his office in the gate house, a building that is still in use. Around 1958 the camp closed down and two years after that the land was purchased by the Marchioness.

In 1986 a reunion for the Old Comrades Association of the Royal Tank Regiments was organised by a local resident, Mrs Gillian Nassau, and the veterans were invited to visit the Centre. At teatime they spontaneously took a collection amongst themselves and gave the Centre £350. The veterans apparently told the then Chief Executive Dorothy Beaumont, "We're very glad you are doing something better here than we were".

Not long after the purchase of the land three architects were shown round the site by Lady Dufferin and Judge Maude, followed finally by a fourth firm that had been found by Bochenek and Peake. In January 1961 this last firm was chosen to be probably the most suitable and the proposal was agreed by the Committee that "Lady Dufferin and Judge Maude be requested to instruct the architects Crabtree & Associates to prepare preliminary plans and perspective drawings". These drawings were presented at the next meeting in March by Mr Crabtree and his associate Mr Senkowsky at the end of which it was decided that building would begin without unnecessary delay and be carried out in stages as funds became available.

Discussions continued throughout 1961 and in October Mr Senkowski was instructed to design Phase 1, the Central Block (Block 1) and also Block 19, this being the bungalow, estimated to cost in the region of £100 000, and to submit the plans to the local council. It had been suggested by the Marchioness at one stage that this bungalow should be named after Bochenek. The latter declined the honour however, saying that she felt it might give the public the wrong impression. She also felt that it would not be appropriate to have her name associated with any structure that was not part of the Centre  itself. The bungalow, later named Panorama, was to be built on the periphery of the site. Peake agreed and it was decided that a small plaque bearing Bochenek's name as founder should be placed instead in the main entrance of the Centre where it can be seen still.

In May 1962 after going out to tender it was decided to place the contract with Messrs Perryman, builders from Paddock Wood, who were instructed to proceed with both the building of Block 1 and Block 19 for the amount of £320 000.

Building began on the 4 June. The somewhat stark bungalow by today's standards and the administration block were the first two buildings to be erected on the site. The door seen on the left appears to have opened into the garage but later alterations removed the door for vehicles and the fence, seen here in the photograph of Bochenek in her wheelchair, which was probably taken soon after she and Peake moved into Panorama in December 1962.

Although the head office of the charity was established at Crowborough at this time, meetings of the Committee continued to take place at Hans Crescent and later at Warwick Road. No doubt the members of the Committee who lived in London did not relish the idea of travelling down to Sussex at regular intervals.

The Bungalow 'Panorama' in 2012 from the front

Cecilia Bochenek outside the bungalow 'Panorama' circa 1962. The photograph of the site of the first ward buildings was taken in 1964. Bochenek's invalid car is seen on the drive to 'Panorama' viewed in the distance.

It was not until March 1963 that a Deed of Gift was drawn up and the 12 ½ acres of the old camp now known as Maureen Dufferin Place were given by the Marchioness to the Centre "together with all the buildings erected or in the course of erection thereon". Before this, in 1961, building permission had been granted and preliminary groundwork, possibly demolition of the old Medical Centre and other old buildings, had begun on the bungalow. The Marchioness, it appears, had given permission for this early building work before the parcel of land was made over formally.

After completion of the bungalow and administration block, progress came to a halt as available funds had run out. In June 1963 the architect Mr Senkowsky informed the Centre that he was leaving Crabtree and setting up on his own. The Committee decided to re-appoint him as architect to the Centres. Some money had to be spent on clearing more derelict buildings left behind by the military and plans were drawn up to re-start building in the autumn if possible, depending on support from subscribers. It was decided to go out to tender for the shell of the central block and the first patients' courtyard, although it would be explained to the competing contractors that building operations would be phased.

In February 1964 the Committee instructed Mr Senkowsky to negotiate a firm contract with the builders, Perrymans, for the building of the shell of the treatment block, the shell of the patients' wing for eight patients and a temporary road, providing the cost did not exceed £880 000. This contract was known as Stage 1 of Phase 2. By October it had been decided that every effort should be made to go ahead with more building but to do so would require approximately £2.6 million at a time when the available funds stood at £1.4 million, half of which was already committed. Bochenek recorded in the minutes that "Sir Edwin Leather and Sir Hugh Dawson kindly agreed to approach the Manager of Barclays Bank, Holborn in the matter of a loan." In due course agreement for a loan was obtained using the buildings and site as security. At this point it was decided to instruct Perrymans to complete their contract for Phase 2, this being the internal completion of the treatment block, Blocks 2 and 3 together with the access road and retaining wall, the boiler house, the water tower and other ancillary external works. Mr Senkowsky was now asked to prepare drawings for Phase 3 and shortly afterwards was given instructions to tell the builders and quantity surveyors to proceed.

Unfortunately unforeseen problems now arose with the builders. Perrymans had run into severe financial difficulties in June 1964 and although it had been decided that they should continue with the work for as long as possible, a few weeks later they went into liquidation with substantial debts. Contracts were put out to tender again and in due course Messrs Llewellyn & Sons of Eastbourne were appointed to complete Phase 2, Stages 1 and 2, and to proceed with Phase 3 at a total cost of £1.5 million. A statement produced by the quantity surveyors in December 1965 detailing the approximate overall cost of building these first three phases of the Centre, albeit with a number of caveats, was £3.4 million.

In 1965 a House Committee was established, the purpose of which was to decide on the interior decorations and furnishings. Sir Edwin Leather took the chair, a decision he may have regretted as the colour and length of curtains, the type of seat covers to be attached to chairs, the colour, thickness and extent of carpeting and the design of wash basins were debated and disputed by the ladies.

By the end of the second meeting Sir Edwin employed the time-honoured formula of declaring the meeting a great success, adding that he saw no reason to call another in the immediate future at which point he handed over the reins to Primrose, Countess Cadogan. One more meeting took place in May 1966 chaired by the Countess when a number of controversial matters were discussed. By then however the relationship between the group from Belgravia, whose ideas on interior design were considered somewhat elaborate and the Centre's Executive, who favoured a more functional decor, was becoming strained and future deliberations appear to have been taken over by the newly established Finance and General Purposes Committee. Soon after this the London ladies departed the scene.

In due course function prevailed over art, financial considerations being an important factor in the decision-making process. Bochenek realised that at that stage it was very difficult to predict the income that would be generated once the Centre opened and although she and Peake had done their best to forecast the running costs in the early stages, this forecast owed more to hope and inspired guesswork than to detailed financial analysis. The interior of the new buildings therefore reflected the rather stark atmosphere of post-war utilitarianism when viewed by a modern observer in contrast to the more comfortable homely environment that they had in mind for the Centre originally and which is the case today.

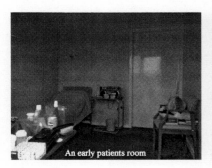
An early patients room

An ensuite patient's room in 2012

Just as the patient's rooms, all of which had easy access to the patients' courtyards, reflected this functional approach so also did the treatment areas, which were designed along very similar lines under the auspices of Dr Peake in particular, as medical adviser.

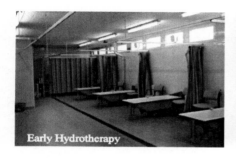
Early Hydrotherapy

Occupational Therapy

The early version of a form of hydrotherapy is particularly revealing, indeed innovative, and perhaps more reminiscent of the communal baths often found in English boarding schools of that period rather than the therapeutic environment found in the spa towns of Tunbridge Wells or Harrogate.

An interesting feature of the original building was the main staircase. Designed to assist rehabilitation each step was low and central rails were  placed to allow people to pass easily when both needed rail support. Dr Ivan Williams, the former consultant rheumatologist at Tunbridge Wells, who succeeded Douglas Woolf as Medical Director of the Centre in 1989, tells an interesting tale that was current in the 1970s about a method used to encourage a reluctant patient to use the stairs. Apparently either Bochenek or Peake would place a pound note at the top and then tell the patient it was theirs' if they managed to ascend the steps. It seems that the drain on the Centre's financial resources was not excessive. The staircase featured prominently at the time of the opening ceremony when the assembled company were on it to see HRH Princess Margaret unveil the Wedgwood plaque recording the occasion.

By April 1966 it became clear that the new builders were unable to achieve the original date for completion owing to a shortage of materials. It was therefore decided to arrange the official opening in October. Llewellyns promised to have the buildings completed by the end of July and after some discussion in Committee it was agreed that Princess Margaret would be approached and asked to open the Centre in the second part of October. The buildings were finally taken over at completion on the 26 September 1966.

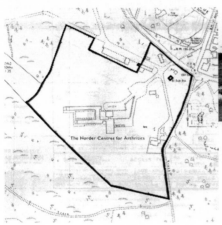

The first ward and treatment block seen as they were in 1966 at the time of opening of the Centre. Every patient's room opened onto a terrace. On the right is seen part of the retaining wall with a car standing on the main drive.

The plan shows the buildings that had been constructed by the time the Centre opened in 1966. The bungalow, Panorama, built and occupied by Bochenek and Peake in 1962, was situated with its own drive and garden to the south-east of the main buildings on the edge of the forest. The central treatment and smaller administrative blocks are seen with the two wings containing patient's rooms extending west towards the left, enclosing the first of the courtyards. The retaining wall extends east or to the right from the junction of the administrative and central blocks and curves down towards the main drive where it remains today.

Bochenek had put her proposals on staffing this first stage of the building to the Committee in February 1964. She stressed that the first patients would be people of working age who would be severely disabled but not bed-ridden. She intended to provide electrically propelled chairs of the "Sley-Ride" type for those who could not walk at all. No member of staff would be allowed to lift a patient and therefore "Hoyer lifts" would have to be provided in adequate numbers. She envisaged that these would soon pay for themselves by the saving on staff salaries and prevention of injuries to patients and staff.

She had, she said, discussed nursing requirements with a state registered nurse (SRN) and this nurse advised that for the first 20 patients there should be one attendant for every four or five patients. She thought that three of these should be SRNs, one in charge of the nurses and patients, one to be a deputy for relief purposes and one for night duty. At night there should also be a state enrolled nurse (SEN) or a nursing assistant. However Bochenek and Peake based on their "own experience in hospitals with arthritic patients" did not think an SRN was necessary at night. The remaining nursing staff, other than the three SRNs, could be SENs or nursing auxiliaries "or even women with nursing experience but no qualifications". Three or four orderlies would be needed for general duties throughout the Centre.

A physiotherapist would be needed but apparently Dr Peake's "special qualifications and experience would enable her to give the treatment" although it was stressed that this additional service should not be expected from any medical superintendent as a matter of course. A similar rider was applied to the paragraph regarding the Department of Creative Occupation where it was pointed out that "the present administrator (Bochenek), as the committee is aware, has special qualifications enabling her to run the department" assuming other duties did not encroach too much on her time. A cook and assistant cook and at least one kitchen maid would be needed for the first 20 patients and a porter-cum-handyman and gardener would also be required. It was envisaged that an almoner would attend for a few sessions each week and it was hoped that some voluntary workers would be found although this was not to be relied upon. Staffing in general led to some difficulties particularly with regard to finding nurses to cover at night. Most of the staff in the early days were part-time but some were resident at the Centre. A night nurse resigned as she could not sleep in the day because of the noise from the Centre. Peake drew attention to the need for sound-proofing the night nurses' sleeping quarters from the everyday noise in the Centre when the planned extension of the building was carried out. Staff turnover was quite large initially and the first matron left after a year or so as did the second.

At this stage no costs were applied by Bochenek to these proposals. However this establishment appears to have been accepted by the Committee and in February 1966 the cost of staffing for 22 patients was estimated, based it appears on Whitley Council scales, to be £230 000 per annum in today's figures. An additional £120 000 was estimated as being required to run the Centre, the largest component being £53 000 for food at £44 per head per week. The total of £350 000 was considered by the Committee to be somewhat optimistic and it was agreed that an estimated figure of £510 000 should be shown in the accounts.

It is interesting to note that in January 2012, according to *The Daily Telegraph*,[1] using figures compiled by the National Health Service (NHS) information centre and disclosed in the House of Commons regarding spending on food and drink for hospital patients, 30 NHS Trusts spent less than £5 on each "patient meal day", rather less than the £44 per week Bochenek and Peake were proposing to spend in 1966. Several NHS hospitals were spending approximately half the sum that they had suggested for the Centre. One is left with the impression that either Bochenek and Peake were being over generous, which seems unlikely in view of their understandably cautious approach to expenditure, or a number of patients in some of the NHS hospitals of the twenty-first century are being starved. In a leading article in October 2012, *The Daily Telegraph* drew attention to figures provided by the Office for National Statistics that revealed that 43 patients in NHS hospitals last year starved to death and nearly 300 were recorded as being malnourished when they died.[2]

Further Reading

1. Hospitals that feed patients on 90p a meal by James Kirkup, Deputy Political Editor *The Daily Telegraph* 11 January 2012.

2. Nursing care in crisis. Leading article. *The Daily Telegraph* 8 October 2012.

THE OPENING AND FIRST PATIENTS

The official opening of the Horder Centre by Her Royal Highness Princess Margaret, Countess of Snowdon took place in the afternoon of the 27 October 1966. After a good deal of discussion beforehand it was decided that the number of people who should be invited to attend the ceremony would be limited to one hundred. The Marchioness and Countess Cadogan had already made it clear that they would not be able to attend and their absence must have been noted with some surprise and possibly regret by some in view of the importance of the occasion and the major part they had played in the development of the Centre. After the Princess had unveiled the plaque near the top of the main staircase, the guests who had been standing on the stairs and on the ground floor separated into small groups "each in charge of a marshal", this no doubt reflecting the chairman's background as an Air Chief Marshal. They then toured the buildings after which the whole party took tea in the dining room. These arrangements apparently went off very satisfactorily and in due course Sir Walter expressed his thanks to everyone who had helped.

The Wedgwood Plaque

Lady Cadogan had arranged for the dedication plaque to be ready for the opening ceremony after consulting Her Royal Highness. This plaque was in two parts with a separate inscription section in case the date had to be changed unexpectedly. She had visited Wedgwood to organise this and negotiated a favourable price. The gilt frames and mounts were given free. Today (2012) this plaque is mounted in the entrance hall of the administration block not far from its original position. The staircase however is now a less impressive structure, having been replaced and reduced in size when a hydrotherapy pool was built in 1986.

The Crowborough edition of the *Sussex Express and County Herald* gave considerable prominence to the opening on its front page that week. A photograph of Bochenek and Peake welcoming the Princess was shown, together with one of the actual unveiling of the plaque. Mrs Cheryl Balchin from Bristol presented a bouquet of orchids. The proceedings were then opened by the Reverend Green the Rector of St John's Church nearby, with a prayer at the special request of Her Royal Highness, for the bereaved of Aberfan. The terrible disaster at the Welsh colliery had occurred just a week before.

Cecilia Bochenek greets Her Royal Highness PrincessMargaret, Countess of Snowdon with Air Chief Marshall Sir Walter Cheshire and Joyce Peake behind before the opening ceremony.

In his welcome address the chairman Sir Walter Cheshire said the opening of the Centre was the culmination of the work of many people but primarily that of Cecilia Bochenek who had launched the idea around 1952. In her reply Princess Margaret remarked on the homely atmosphere and the ideal setting for this exciting pioneer work that would encourage patients to regain some of their lost independence.

She drew attention to the unique staircase, on which the assembled company were standing, which was intended as a practising ground for patients. She acknowledged that with the exception of the medical department the internal decorations and soft furnishings had been chosen by Maureen, Marchioness of Dufferin and Ava and Primrose, Countess Cadogan. She thanked the Marchioness for her gift of the wonderful site and for all her hard work for the Centre over the past 7 years. Thanks were also due to all those who had the cause at heart and in particular Miss Bochenek. She then formally opened the Centre and then toured the Centre staying for tea afterwards, cutting a special cake that had been baked for the occasion. The photograph shows her with Dr Peake and a nurse talking to two of the first patients who had been admitted to the Centre a few days before.

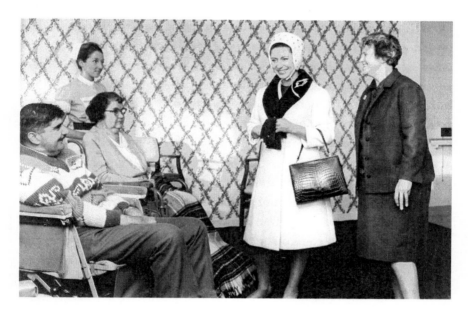

An associated article in the newspaper described how Princess Margaret had visited the building work in April 1965 in her capacity as President when she had been accompanied by the donor of the site, the Marchioness of Dufferin and Ava. The Centre was depicted as providing a new and rather subtle psychological approach combined with modern physical treatment, which would make a stay in the Centre highly significant and dynamic. This would make it a turning point in the lives of arthritic patients many of whom had been told that "nothing more can be done". It was noted that the future requirement for funds would continue to grow and that money would be needed to subsidise the operating costs.

A few weeks after the opening, the Medical Director presented her interim report on the first month's running of the Centre. Two days before the official opening six patients had been admitted. Four more were expected shortly but already it was proving difficult to obtain funds to support these patients from local authorities, or as Peake put it in her report "to persuade the local authorities to accept financial responsibility". She intended to approach the South East Metropolitan Regional Hospital Board again when a few patients had been discharged in a better condition than on admission.

Employing orderlies had proved to be unsatisfactory, so qualified nurses, state registered or enrolled, were being employed instead. The overall wages bill, excluding the salary of the director (Bochenek) and the office staff, but including Peake's salary, was approximately £130 000 per annum. Peake estimated the costs would rise to around £160 000 when the full complement of 22 patients had been admitted as this would require a small increase in staff numbers. The present charge for patients was £200 per week and therefore with 22 patients in the Centre income was estimated at £230 000 a year. The expenditure on meals for patients was, "as she had predicted, two pounds fifteen shillings", £44 a week in 2012.

In January 1966 a sub-committee had been set up known as the Finance and General Purposes committee. It is very difficult to distinguish between the work of this sub-committee and the Committee of Management as both the membership and the functions of the two seem to have been very similar. Discussion took place initially as to whether the sub-committee had executive functions or not but in practice it appears to have assumed these anyway. It does appear to have been concerned with greater detail on financial matters on which it reported to the Committee of Management at intervals. Bochenek and Peake of course attended both. The minutes of both these committees provide a useful record of the Centre's activity and finances at that time. Until the middle of 1967 meetings of both had been held at 10 Warwick Road in London but from June onwards meetings of the Finance and General Purposes committee appear to have been held in Crowborough, whilst the Committee of Management continued in London. By 1971 the meetings of the two became in practice interchangeable and all took place at Crowborough.

The wages paid to nursing staff in 1967 are of interest. Matron received £14 000 per annum and a Staff Nurse £11 000. Nursing aides who were part-time received £3.80 an hour. It appears that Peake adhered to the current Whitley Council scales. In June, Bochenek announced the good news that the South East Regional Hospital Board had agreed to pay for a maximum of five patients at the Centre on a regular basis and in August, Peake enlarged on this by adding that Dr Robinson from the Board had called at the Centre and confirmed that they had agreed to pay £320 a week for the five patients admitted from the Board's area. All hospitals in the region had been informed. In 1969 payment rose to £340 for these patients and local councils agreed to raise their fees to £260 a week from £190.

A report on the first year was drawn up by Peake in October 1967. Of the first five patients, two had been admitted from north London, one from Cheshire, one from Leicester and one from Cornwall. Before the Regional Board agreed to fund five beds, all patients apart from two who funded themselves were paid for by the welfare departments of their local councils. This left a significant shortfall for the Centre. However the contract with the Regional Board in September led to a major improvement. In October all five Regional Board beds were occupied and there were 15 other patients in the Centre near to the limit of 22. The minimum length of stay was three months but when marked improvement was considered to be taking place the council concerned was asked to extend payment and so far Peake said none had refused.

By November, Peake was able to report encouraging clinical results and a number of success stories of patients who had been admitted and then taught to walk again were being published in the press. She described two cases in some detail. One was a young man of 28 with a history of eight years with arthritis who had been in several hospitals. He had become withdrawn and anxious. He suffered from bouts of depression when he thought his progress was too slow but, "a talk with the director (Bochenek), however, invariably puts him on the rails again". After six months she reported that he was walking around the Centre with crutches and joining in all activities. He had started a postal course on book-keeping and the Ministry of Pensions had agreed to supply him with an invalid car giving him mobility at home.

Another was a 54-year-old man with ankylosing spondylitis, a condition which leads to marked stiffness and deformity of the major joints and spine, who had been lying in bed for 18 years before he came to the Centre. As she described the situation "no effort was made in hospital to get him moving, or even sitting up". After 11 months he was able to walk again and could apparently manage a hundred paces with crutches.

These two cases are interesting examples of the approach by Peake and Bochenek to patients with advanced chronic arthritis who had as it were "fallen off the radar" once their acute illness had been treated and for whom no rehabilitation was provided or available. The mainstream hospitals of the National Health Service (NHS) were under pressure as always to clear beds to make way for more admissions and facilities for managing the problems of the severely disabled arthritic patient were rarely provided or available. Such patients were therefore either discharged to nursing homes or cottage hospitals where they remained, cared for but not treated, or sent home to manage as best they could.

Fortunately a number of cine films survive that were taken in the very earliest years of the Centre and one of these from 1968 shows the first patients to be admitted, including the two patients described above. These patients had often been in hospital for many years and were extremely disabled by destructive rheumatoid arthritis in the era before medical advances and joint replacement surgery revolutionised the management of this disease and led to a fundamental change with regard to management of advanced arthritis. They had reached a point where the medical services of the time could do nothing for them other than provide institutional care often in inappropriate surroundings. One woman in her late thirties describes how after contracting rheumatoid arthritis when she was 18 she was eventually sent to a geriatric unit at the age of 25 where she remained until admitted to the Centre. The dramatic beneficial changes achieved with regard to patients' quality of life and mobility following the care they received at the Centre are clearly demonstrated in these old films.

As long ago as 1955 Bochenek had described the aim of the Horder project to a newspaper reporter: "Our first Centre will be neither a home, nor a hospital – rather would it be a sort of shuttle service between home and hospital. We would take patients from hospital after they have had their treatment. They could be discharged sooner than otherwise and that would mean new patients could be accepted sooner at the hospital." At the annual meeting of the Horder Centres Helpers in 1979 Peake was asked "why, if our special treatment was so successful, it could not be written down so that it could be made available to those who, for one reason or another, were not able to be admitted to the Centre?" Peake explained that "this was not feasible as each patient was treated individually and our psychological approach was 'tailored' to the particular needs of the person being treated. One had to start from the position the patient was at, both physically and mentally, and to teach each one that the mental approach to their difficulties was of paramount importance. Some were able to understand this quickly but others took longer and a great deal of patience was called for on the part of the patient and the medical and nursing staff". The question remains however as to whether they had sufficient up-to-date clinical expertise available to provide the multi-disciplinary approach they advocated, something the Marchioness had touched on just before she resigned.

Such a personalised concept of individual patient care was indeed noteworthy at the time they sought to introduce it at Crowborough in the mid 1960s. Lord Horder when he first gave his support to Bochenek and Peake at the beginning had described their idea as not only valuable but original. The successes they achieved almost certainly arose from the intensive personal input and encouragement of their patients, which they provided on an individual basis, rather than from any special concept of medical practice. In addition the ambience of the new building with its delightful setting in the heart of the Ashdown Forest must have provided enormous psychological encouragement for those who had been incarcerated in dreary Victorian buildings that were a common feature of the state-run hospitals of the time, particularly those set aside for the care of those with mental or chronic illness. It would be many years before the NHS was able to replace these old relics of the past with the modern buildings of today. It is unfortunate that the personalised care of patients today, despite all the rhetoric, is still too rarely experienced by the patient with long-term disability.

MORE BUILDING AND FINANCIAL PROBLEMS

Towards the end of 1968 a decision was made to proceed with the next phase of building. Mr Senkowsky had submitted his final account in May and it was hoped this would bring to an end the rather protracted discussions with him over payment of fees, which had arisen partly as a result of problems following the bankruptcy of the builders Perrymans. Frederick Gibberd & Partners were selected as the new architects. Sir Frederick had visited the Centre and was asked to prepare plans. It had been decided that the medical department was much too cramped and a proposal was put forward that some of the staff rooms should be on the ground floor as "it might then be possible for disabled arthritics to be employed on certain staff duties".

In October of the following year the architects supplied a model of their design. Bochenek and Peake considered that this was not in accordance with proposals they had put forward so another meeting was arranged and on this occasion a number of changes were made. The architects had placed the dining room and medical department at the far end of the Centre, presumably at the western end of the present patient's wing, whereas the committee wished it to be in the middle. If this were to be done it was accepted that patients in rooms on the ground floor of the medical department would need a lift to reach the dining room but Bochenek did not see a problem with this as long as the lift could take four wheelchairs at a time. In addition, it was thought the space for the kitchens and dining room would probably need to be three times bigger than in the present design. Parking for chairs in the dining room was required and there should be an exercise yard for patients learning to walk again. Increased office accommodation was needed so that the Director, as Bochenek was now called, would have easy access to the staff and visitors who came to see her. Peake felt that for every three baths in the medical department there should be space for two "rest" beds but she did not think it was essential to provide a pool. The architect said he would prepare new drawings and send five copies to the Director. This was done and in due course these new plans were "approved in principle".

In June 1971 a tender submitted by YJ Lovell (Building) Ltd. was accepted and they were appointed as the main contractors. Building began in August and they anticipated finishing the first phase of the extension by August 1972. This was achieved and in October the architects were instructed to prepare further plans to complete the Centre. The tenders went out in November 1973 and again Lovell was given the contract.

More building started in April 1974. Work was delayed by bad weather and problems with pipes and drains that had been laid imperfectly at the time of earlier building in 1966. There had been significant problems with these in the past and these problems were to loom large over the next few years. In the midst of all this the boiler in Panorama blew up and it was therefore decided to bring forward the plan already in place to connect the heating in the bungalow to the main building. The pipes in the bungalow had to be replaced at the same time.

The Buildings Circa 1980

Building was completed by August 1975 but many defects came to light over the next few months. The drains frequently became blocked once patients moved into the new wing. Patients and staff complained of the smell from the sluices and Bochenek called in the local public health inspector to investigate and report. She and Peake battled on struggling to deal with a number of significant problems with the buildings generally. Architects Hubbard Ford & Partners of Eastbourne were brought in as advisers, as difficulty had been experienced in getting the Centre's architects and other contractors to accept responsibility and correct faults.

In October 1976 following a long discussion about the drainage system, the corridor flooring, faulty expansion joints and rendering, it was decided to ask solicitors to act for the Horder Centre to bring the setbacks with the Phase B buildings to a satisfactory conclusion. Eventually it was accepted that if anything was going to be done to sort all this out, particularly the pipes and drains, the Centre would have to pay for the work itself. A local building firm, ALW Contractors of Crowborough, were employed to undertake the pipe and drain work at a cost of £180 000. This work was done between October 1977 and March 1978. The final cost of the extensions to the original 1966 buildings, excluding the above remedial work, was £1.9 million at today's equivalent.

For the first four years, when there were only 22 beds, the occupancy levels had been high and increases in the fees paid by the Regional Hospital Board and local councils had in the main helped to keep pace with inflation. The first patients were aged between 16 and 60, with six or seven in the younger age group. Several stayed for over a year and some for up to four years with a turnover of around 20 a year. By 1971 however a number of rooms remained unoccupied and more elderly patients were being admitted. In a paper to the committee in August of that year Bochenek and Peake put forward their views as to why this was so.

The nucleus of young patients who had been long stay had eventually left "happily because they were all well enough to leave and start work". Over the past year an unusually high number had left, against the advice of the Medical Director. Some of these patients were considered unsuitable because of physical or mental illness that had not been disclosed or only became apparent after admission. Others were "too old mentally to benefit from our treatment". In addition it appeared that the local authorities were under increasing financial pressure and in some cases refused to pay for what was known as Part 3 accommodation at the Horder Centre. The

Centre was funding each patient to the sum of £160 or so each week to supplement payments from the local authorities or the Regional Board. In addition enquiries had shown that young people were reluctant to come to the Centre at all, let alone stay for three months.

By now Bochenek was again broadcasting information on the radio about the Centre and she persuaded Franklin Englemen to visit the Centre with his team from "Down Your Way", a BBC programme that was very popular at the time. From time to time letters and leaflets were sent to rheumatologists, consultants in physical medicine, orthopaedic surgeons and medical social workers. An article by Peake had been published in the *British Medical Journal* and *The Lancet* to which there was no response. The Secretary of State for Health, Sir Keith Joseph, had been sent a letter asking him to direct any Regional Board in whose area there might be a patient who had been referred to the Centre and who was waiting for admission to pay the Centre accordingly. Following a long delay the letter was acknowledged "but nothing more happened". A second letter received the reply "The matter is under consideration".

The conclusion reached by Bochenek and Peake was that they had to broaden the Centre's admission policy to take long-term patients, with priority being given to younger ones. They were clearly worried that they would end up with too many permanent elderly residents needing more medical and nursing care than younger patients. The long-term elderly would be provided with rooms at the lower level and given their own dining room and lounge. It was also decided that they would require classes by themselves for relaxing and carrying out remedial exercises. To put into practice this policy change they intended to add consultant geriatricians to the list of correspondents.

It was hoped that the 1972 White Paper *The National Health Service Reorganisation Bill*, which was then being piloted through Parliament by Sir Keith Joseph to be introduced in 1974, would proceed quickly and that this would lead to improvement. For a while this seemed to be the case but by the end of 1975 difficulty was again being experienced in getting funds from the new area health authorities (AHAs) and local authorities. The Act had replaced the regional health boards with 14 regional health authorities (RHAs) who were responsible for strategy, building and staffing together with allocation of resources to 90 new AHAs. Supervised by these AHAs were 192 District Management Teams (DMTs). The executive councils that had previously controlled general practice were replaced by 90 family practitioner committees (FPCs) and perhaps most controversially, in response to the call that the patient's voice should be heard, community health councils (CHCs) were created. With all this going on in the National Health Service (NHS) the concerns of a small rehabilitation centre is Sussex were understandably of limited concern to those responsible for introducing the new management structures.

By 1977 financial problems were becoming more serious. Peake told the committee in April that their chief concern was to get the beds filled and to help achieve this she was writing to orthopaedic surgeons and physicians throughout the country telling them about the facilities available for treating patients at the Centre. In February a meeting had taken place at Crowborough with Sir John Donne, Chairman of the RHA at that time and Dr Porter the Regional Medical Officer to discuss ways in which it was hoped the authority might be able to help the Centre obtain finance for patients. Nothing seems to have resulted from this.

A visit was made in June 1977 by the Secretary of State for Health, David Ennals following two visits by Eastbourne CHC which, according to reports in the local press, described the Centre as "very austere" and also claimed patients were not given enough food. Mr Ennals said he was disturbed to see that the Centre was under used. He had seen some of the criticism and it surprised him very much. He thought it had "enormous potential. It certainly does not seem to have an atmosphere of a prison as someone suggested". He added that inspectors from the Department of Health and Social Security (DHSS) who had visited the Centre could not understand the criticism either. He inspected the new extension, which would increase the number of rooms to allow for 40 patients, although only 18 were present at that time, partly due to cutbacks in local authority spending. He promised to set up a working party to explore ways in which the DHSS could help with payment for patients.

In 1979 the subject of food was discussed again and Peake spoke then in some detail about it. "Food is good but not fancy. Patients understand that they cannot have luxury food on £33 a week. They must buy something themselves. Fish is very expensive. People who pay can have it if they pay £2.10 extra." It appears therefore that the amount spent on food for each patient had been considerably reduced since her estimate of £44 a week was laid before the committee in 1966.

Sadly, little practical assistance seems to have come following this visit by the minister, with the customary promise to set up a working party, in spite of an exchange of correspondence between Bochenek and the DHSS. Bochenek's idea by now was that the Centre would "maintain its charitable status with an independent committee of management and that the state, through the DHSS, would be responsible for payment of maintenance of patients and staff salaries". Such a vision can be seen to have been little more than a forlorn hope.

Throughout this time Bochenek and Peake had managed to keep up the income from donations, charitable trusts and appeals and at the end of 1977 the accounts still showed a healthy balance and the overdraft facility arranged with the bank had not been used. However it was becoming only too clear to both of them that without more patients, the future looked bleak.

In August 1978 at a meeting of the committee Sir Derek Gilbey reported that recently he and the Vice-chairman Mr Baker had met the new Regional Medical Officer, Dr Malcolm Forsythe and discussed what help the DHSS, through the Region, might be able to give to the Centre. During the discussion it became clear that Dr Forsythe considered that it would be very difficult to help the Centre in any substantial way without absorbing it into the NHS. One problem he said was a discrepancy in the salaries being paid at the Centre compared to those in the NHS. Another problem was that staff in the treatment department did not include qualified physiotherapists. This brought a riposte from Peake who "could only think Dr Forsythe was under the impression that our unqualified staff in the treatment department were being paid professional rates" thus missing the point. She would write to him to set the record straight. Dr Maw, who had joined the committee in 1973, commented that if the Region were to provide help they would see it as a takeover bid whereas he thought it was essential that the Centre retain its independence. Peake then explained that what she and Bochenek wanted was for the Centre to be classed as supra-regional so that patients would come from any part of the country. The doctors on the committee thought that it was very unlikely that in difficult financial times the NHS would support an independent hospital in this way. A final suggestion by Dr Forsythe that the Centre might merge with another organisation such as the Cheshire Homes "was agreed to be out of the question".

Bochenek then informed the committee about an article that had appeared in a magazine, *British Medicine*, by Lord George Brown criticising the way in which the NHS was being run. Peake had written to him, and George Brown, who lived in Sussex, had visited the Centre in August and had then apparently written to Mr Ennals. In his reply in March 1979 Ennals made it clear that "the NHS is under considerable financial stress and the situation is likely to continue for a long time". A lively discussion took place around this time on Capital Radio (independent radio station for London) between George Brown and Dr Forsythe in which the problems of the Centre were aired.

George Brown forwarded a copy of the Secretary of State's letter to Peake. In a reply thanking him, Peake wrote: "Short of taking over the Centre completely, it seems the DHSS can see no way to assist with the financing of patients. The South East Region has indicated that it would be reluctant to take over the Horder Centre and our committee would not in any case consider it."

However more was to come in due course from these contacts with the Region. In early 1980 Dr Forsythe asked Mr Michael Devas, an orthopaedic surgeon at Hastings to contact Mr Baker. Following this initiative Devas and I (the author), who had recently joined him at Hastings, had lunch at the Centre on the 22 July with Sir Derek Gilbey, the Vice-chairman Mr Baker, Bochenek and Peake and other members of the committee. Reasons for and against the establishment of orthopaedic surgery at the Centre were discussed and it emerged, to the surprise of some committee members, that the Centre's architects had already been asked to prepare revised plans for the completion of the Centre as outline planning permission for this was about to expire. The proposed plan it seems was not only for a possible operating theatre unit but also a new bungalow for the Director and Medical Director.

The cost of the operating theatre complex was estimated to be in the region of £3.6 million and that of the bungalow, access road and link to the existing buildings £400 000. It was duly agreed that the architects would be instructed to submit preliminary plans to Wealden Council for the bungalow before the existing outline planning permission expired. It was also pointed out that should the whole project go ahead plans for the bungalow would need to be greatly modified. In October 1980 a planning application was granted by Wealden District Council for permission to build "New accommodation for the Director and Medical Director". No mention was made of an operating theatre.

It had so happened that in 1968 the then Chairman, Richard Medley, a solicitor, had written to both Bochenek and Peake to clarify their terms of employment and in particular their age for retirement which had been fixed at 75 years old. By 1980 Bochenek was 74 and Peake 77, so she should have retired therefore under the terms of the agreement. It had also been agreed that they would continue to live at the Centre after retirement, rent free with heating and lighting provided, if they so wished. The building of the new bungalow was understandably a matter of considerable importance to them.

At the end of August 1980 another meeting took place to which Dr Forsythe and Mr Devas were invited to reconsider the question of surgery. Peake was unwell although she sent a note in which she expressed her reservations. Bochenek opened the meeting by explaining that "it had been called to discuss with Dr Forsythe the possibility of Regional cooperation and financial backing in the running of the operating theatre if the facilities were provided by the Horder Centre". The Centre had £2.1 million in hand and it was expected that the cost of the surgical unit would be in the region of £4.2 million.

The discussion ebbed and flowed. Dr Forsythe asked why two operating theatres were proposed when one would appear to be sufficient in view of the number of beds available. He also asked whether it was envisaged that at some time the whole Centre might be used for surgical care, demonstrating a remarkable degree of prescience in view of much later developments. He received the reply "not initially". A great deal of the time was spent discussing the requirements of the NHS regarding staffing ratios, safety, medical cover and building design. Mr Devas gave advice on surgical matters and Dr Maw underlined the need "to sell the idea locally [meaning Tunbridge Wells] so that the orthopaedic surgeons would be motivated to provide the cover we should need". The meeting ended with a decision to undertake further discussion and Devas was recorded as saying that he hoped the Centre would become the South East Centre for joint replacement.

Following this meeting Devas wrote to Baker, the Vice-chairman, who he knew quite well, encouraging him to consider a proposal to build a single theatre with a small emergency one doubling as a plaster room. He believed that Dr Forsythe at the region was willing to support "some such scheme". However Devas was on the point of retiring and would not have been involved in developing the project leaving me to take it on. Following our visit in June we had discussed the concept together in some detail. At that time I had only recently arrived in the area from London where I had been working as a consultant at St George's Hospital for the past six years and I had a good deal of work to do at my base in Hastings. From what I had seen of the Centre on our visit and from subsequent enquiry I did not consider that the scheme was feasible under the present management. However I did think that if circumstances changed it might be possible to seize the opportunity to develop its potential for surgery and thus help to reduce the ever-increasing waiting time for joint replacement surgery, a national problem and a particular one on the South Coast with its large population of elderly people. For the time being I put it to the back of my mind until in due course, as will be seen, that opportunity did arise.

Following a further discussion in committee in October 1980 it became evident that the scheme for developing surgery at the Centre would not have the support of the surgeons in Tunbridge Wells. It was thought to be impractical for surgeons from farther afield to operate there, the running costs would be very high, and if the facilities were under used, prohibitive. At the beginning of December 1980 a decision was made by the Chairman, Vice-chairman, Director and Medical Director that they would not carry on with the project.

THE DEATH OF CECILIA
BOCHENEK AND HER LEGACY

At the end of a long and what turned out to be an unrewarding discussion in October 1980 regarding the possibility of surgery at the Centre, Peake again raised the matter of the proposed new bungalow. She emphasised that when she and Bochenek retired they would need a bungalow close to the Centre so that they could release their present one, Panorama, for another doctor. The committee agreed to ask the architects to revise the plans to the satisfaction of Bochenek and Peake. Dr Maw, supporting the project, felt that if the Centre was taking a new direction, although he did not describe what this was to be, they would need advice from someone who knew the problems of disabled and arthritic people in particular. "Who better to provide this than the present director and medical director?" In the long term, if not required for accommodation, it could be used as a unit for trying out new aids for disabled people.

Peake's Patch in 1982

Work on the new bungalow started in August 1981 after the building contract had been placed with YJ Lovell at a cost of £320 000. The cost included more work on the drains in a further attempt to overcome the perennial problem of blockages, which had plagued the Centre since the time of the first building in the 1960s. The new bungalow was completed in 1982 and Peake then moved into what became known as "Peake's Patch" for the rest of her life.

Sadly Cecilia Bochenek did not live to see the new bungalow. She had not been well for much of 1980 and towards the end of that year she became seriously ill. It soon became clear that her illness was terminal. Cecilia Dorothea Bochenek died aged 75 from cancer after a short final illness on the 22 April 1981 in Ticehurst House, a private clinic in East Sussex. A Requiem Mass was held at St Mary's Catholic Church Crowborough on 29 April and was followed by private cremation according to her wishes.

The achievements of Cecilia Bochenek, assisted loyally throughout by Joyce Peake who had joined her in the enterprise at the very beginning, were indeed remarkable. Starting with almost nothing apart from her indomitable will and determination she had raised close to five million pounds in today's terms to build her Centre and although arrangements were made to draw on help from the bank from time to time it seems these loans were never taken up. Over the years however pragmatism triumphed over ambition. Her initial concept envisaged many Horder Centres spread around the country and in particular one to help the very young who had experienced the destruction of their childhood through the ravages of Still's disease from which she herself had suffered. As time passed it became clear to her that this early concept was unrealistic although the development of the Horder Helpers was an attempt to provide this service in an achievable form.

The motivation that sustained her and Joyce Peake throughout was exceptional. They had an unshakeable belief that their treatment methods were "special". Peake undertook to provide physiotherapy and fell out with a number of more experienced practitioners of that art who showed reluctance to adopt what she often called "our methods". There was much talk of the importance of the psychological approach to managing illness and indeed Bochenek often spoke of her training in psychology, although whether she undertook any formal instruction is impossible to say now. In 1971 a Dr Christine Pickard, a medical journalist of the time, writing in

The Yorkshire Evening Post described with some considerable insight how Bochenek went about her task. Following an interview, the writer declared: "She is a trained psychologist who concentrates on helping her patients out of their emotional difficulties; she bullies them out of the depressions which could set their progress back. Her affliction means that the patients cannot possibly fail to respond to her." Bochenek apparently told the writer: "Everyone knows that pain disappears if they are involved in something really interesting like a good gossip on the telephone. I try and get people into this state of mind all the time - make them interested."

With this philosophy Bochenek and Peake can be seen to be ahead of their time although the way they went about their task in practice now

seems somewhat dated and in many ways eccentric. The importance of encouraging a patient to take control of their lives again following debilitating illness or as a consequence of advancing years was not at that time universally acknowledged within the professions. Michael Devas who accompanied me on that early abortive visit in 1980 had a useful aphorism. "Bed rest is rehabilitation for the grave" he would say as he encouraged a reluctant or anxious patient to get up and walk after surgery. Bochenek echoed these words with: "We are not trying to make life easy for them [patients], we are trying to make them do more for themselves." Not for her the dependency culture which sadly has become such a feature of modern day life.

She and Peake were not short of innovative ideas and not slow to introduce them. When the first bungalow, Panorama, was opened in 1962 they opened the building, although it was their home, for others to see the special adaptations such as easily manipulated door handles and taps, basins shaped so that they could be approached by

people in wheelchairs and light switches place at a low level. In 1960, Peake announced the invention of an electrical gadget that people could use if they fell in their home or were unable to move after a fall. The device was subjected to a trial by the welfare department of the London County Council and six patients were recruited to take part. This is possibly the first appearance of a calling device for disabled people, something which nowadays is used quite commonly. In the summer of 1966 the journal of *The Disabled Drivers' Motor Club* published an article describing an adaptation to a car seat that had been invented by Bochenek to help her get in and out of her Invacar. The device was adopted by the Ministry of Health and a number of Invacars were modified accordingly. The photograph was taken when Princess Margaret made a private visit in 1965, when she asked for a demonstration of this gadget; Bochenek had her Invacar parked near the entrance so that she could show it to the Princess.

There is no doubt that Bochenek was a hard taskmaster. There are numerous examples in the early history of the Centre of how she refused to tolerate any attempt to divert her from her chosen path. Those who disagreed with her soon experienced her displeasure and social status was no guard against her wrath. Matrons came and went and staff turnover was higher than ideal. At times this led to unfortunate consequences, and the loss of support of the wealthy and socially powerful friends in London who supported the venture in the early days undoubtedly made life more difficult than it might have been, although it does not appear to have prevented Bochenek from continuing to raise considerable sums of money. Reminiscing in 2011, Dr Colin Ruck whose nearby practice had included Bochenek and Peake as patients, said of her, "Miss Bochenek had many admirers but not many friends".

The relationship between the Centre and the National Health Service (NHS) was an interesting one. In a newspaper article in 1955 Bochenek was quoted as saying "there will be no aid from the National Health Service. This scheme is quite new. We are the only one in the country and I believe the only one in the world, but we have to have some time before we can get help from the health service". Another article in 1957 described Peake as saying that many people asked why the Centres were not set up and run by the NHS. She had replied: "Yes, the Health Service ought to do this, but it won't or can't afford it - we do feel however, that we do need complete freedom to develop new ideas so that the first of our Centres may serve as a working model of what can and ought to be done. Time alone will show whether or not our Centres will eventually fall into the framework of the National Health Service".

It would appear from these early comments that the possibility of the Centre becoming part of the NHS had been at the back of their minds from the beginning. By 1977, however, that possibility was being considered seriously. The talks between Bochenek and Peake with officers of the Regional Health Authority and the Secretary of State for Health, David Ennals led on to the talks with Dr Forsythe that have been described. Dr Maw once asked in committee what guarantee the Centre would have, if incorporation with the NHS came about, that the original aims would be maintained. Peake replied that the only hope was that enough medical support would be available to put pressure on "the administrators", by which she presumably meant those managing the NHS, to keep the Centre running in the present way. Although the way the Centre was run was to change radically in the 1980s and beyond, the underlying aim of restoring independence to those afflicted by arthritis or disorders of the musculo-skeletal system was preserved and continues alongside and supporting the NHS, to this day. Today's independent Horder Centre and the state-run NHS have developed a symbiotic relationship to the mutual benefit of both.

In July 1979, at the 15th annual meeting of the Horder Helpers at Crowborough, the Teddington representative, Teddington being one of only two branches that sent representatives to that meeting, the other being Sutton, said they had been asked to enquire about the future of the Centre after Miss Bochenek and Dr Peake were no longer actively engaged in policy making and organisation. What was recorded in answer could almost have been written as a valediction of their work and reads as follows:

"It was pointed out that from the beginning there had been doctors and consultants serving on the committee of management and the medical council. These were experts in their own field of physical medicine or rheumatology who were very concerned to preserve the identity of the Horder Centre as an establishment meeting a very great need which was not met elsewhere. The Horder Centre had been registered as a nursing home from the outset and this fact would allow some flexibility should it be required, without in any way affecting the charitable status of the organisation. The members were assured that, while Miss Bochenek and Dr

Peake had devoted their lives personally to the setting up and to the running of the Centre the organisation had been built in the full expectation that the Horder Centre for Arthritics would be able to fulfil its role for a long time ahead. Naturally, neither they nor anyone else could see how circumstances might change in the future and it would be unrealistic to try to forecast the exact nature of future development."

There can be little doubt that without the determination and drive of these two remarkable women the Horder Centre would not exist today. Whilst others have built on their work and that of the small band of supporters who worked so hard in those first thirty years to turn their vision into reality, they were the underlying driving force. That is their legacy.

Not long after Cecilia Bochenek's death, Dorothy Beaumont who had recently been appointed administrator and secretary to the Centre, with Dr Peake continuing as Medical Director, wrote an appeal letter at the end of which she sought to provide reassurance concerning the future of the charity. After notifying potential benefactors of the recent death of the principal founder she wrote: "Although Cecilia Bochenek is no longer with us, her work and example live on. The committee of management have arranged for the administration of the Centre to be in the hands of the two who had worked shoulder to shoulder with our late director for many years. In appealing to you for funds we look with confidence to the future of the Centre and hope that you will be able to help us". It was time to move on.

PART 2

1981 – 2011

THE INTRODUCTION OF SURGERY

*And as a wise man has said, no one has
ever done anything great or useful by
listening to the voices from without.*

Florence Nightingale, Notes on Nursing; 1860

Chronology 1981 – 2011

1981 – Dorothy Beaumont becomes administrator following Cecilia Bochenek's death.

1982- NHS restructuring. Area Health Authorities replaced by 192 District Health Authorities.

1982 – Dr Douglas Woolf appointed Medical Director on Dr Joyce Peake's retirement.

1983 – Visit by HRH Princess Margaret on 20 October.

1983 – Denys Milne CBE appointed Chairman.

1983 – First Cecilia Bochenek Memorial Lecture given by Professor Eric Bywaters.

1985 – Discussion between Charles Gallannaugh and Dr Malcolm Forsythe regarding the use of Horder Centre facilities for orthopaedic surgery by NHS.

1985 – Medical Director Dr Woolf approached with a proposal to establish hip replacement surgery at the Horder Centre.

1986 – Opening of hydrotherapy pool on 11 December by HRH Princess Margaret.

1987 – Second Cecilia Bochenek Memorial Lecture given by Dr Frank Dudley Hart.

1988 – John Ball appointed Chief Executive in September following Dorothy Beaumont's retirement.

1989 – GP fundholding, NHS Trusts (providers) and District purchasers set up.

1989 – Lene Gurney appointed Senior Nursing Officer on 1 June.

1989 – Dr Douglas Woolf retires in August and Dr Ivan Williams becomes Medical Director.

1989 – Sister Carole Otway appointed first Theatre Superintendent.

1989 – The first hip replacement operation takes place on 28 September.

1990 – Official opening of the Surgical Department on the 25 April by HRH Princess Margaret

1990 – Death of Dr Joyce Peake on 21 May.

1993 – Charles Gallannaugh appointed first Surgical Director. Dr Ivan Williams continues as Medical Director.

1993 – Opening of first out-patient department by HRH Princess Margaret.

1995 – Name change to The Horder Centre for Arthritis.

1995 – RHAs reduced from 14 to 8. DHAs and FHAs merged into 100 Health Authorities.

1996 – The Horder Centre for Arthritis re-registered as a Charitable Company Limited by Guarantee.

1996 – Professor Malcolm Forsythe appointed Chairman.

1996 – Dr Ivan Williams retires as Medical Director and Dr Stewart Torode appointed.

1996 – Opening of Bone Bank.

1996 – Opening of first Therapy Garden by HRH Princess Margaret on 25 October.

1999 – Sir Tim Chessells appointed Chairman.

2000 – Opening of the refurbished out-patient department by HRH Princess Margaret.

2000 – Deaths of Denys Milne and Dr Douglas Woolf.

2001 – Diane Thomas succeeds John Ball as Chief Executive in July.

2002 – Death of HRH Princess Margaret, President of The Horder Centre, on 9 February.

2003 – Opening of the new twin operating theatres.

2009 – Roy Greenhalgh appointed Chairman.

2010 – Start of capital re-development programme.

2011 – Opening of new physiotherapy department by Sally Gunnell OBE.

2011 – Completion of new reception area and refurbishment of patients' rooms and communal areas.

ILLUSTRATIONS AND LEGENDS PART 2

THE HORDER CENTRE IN
THE HEALTH CARE SYSTEM

Following the death of Cecilia Bochenek the Horder Centre entered a new phase of development which would lead to a distinct change in direction during the course of the decade. It is perhaps appropriate therefore to take stock of the Centre's position in the overall system of health care in the country at the start of the ninth decade. The early history of the Centre is of interest in that it demonstrates the establishment of an independent medical organisation at a time when the national and indeed international trends were moving in the opposite direction. In the first half of the twentieth century, before 5 July 1948 when the National Health Service (NHS) was introduced in Britain, a diverse group of authorities were responsible for providing health services.

In 1920 the Consultative Council on Medical and Allied Services produced an interim report for Parliament on the *Future Provision of Medical and Allied Services*, which became known as the *Dawson Report* after its Chairman, Lord Dawson of Penn.[1] The Council had been established under the Ministry of Health Act (1919) and its somewhat pedantic terms of reference were:

"To consider and make recommendations as to the scheme or schemes requisite for the systematised provision of such forms of medical and allied services as should, in the opinion of the Council, be available for the inhabitants of a given area."

The Council of 20 members comprised almost entirely members of the medical profession, and of the four non-medical members, two were Fellows of the Royal Society. It reported to the Minister of Health, Christopher Addison, himself a doctor, and action was taken quickly by the Ministry and local authorities in relation to several matters touched upon in the report. The report was the first attempt to introduce a health service for the country as a whole and indeed introduced ideas at the time that can be seen to form a foundation upon which the later changes introduced in 1948 were based. The underlying philosophy of the Council was summarised briefly at the beginning:

"Any scheme of services must be available for all classes of the community, under conditions to be hereafter determined. In using the word 'available,' we do not mean that the services are to be free; we exclude for the moment the question how they are to be paid for. Any scheme must further be such that it can grow and expand and be adapted to varying local conditions. It must be capable of comprising all those medical services necessary to the health of the people."

In summary their proposals were based on a regional system with domiciliary services provided by doctors, known today as general practitioners, based on a primary health centre similar to the cottage hospitals of today or the recent past. Several of these primary centres would be supported by a secondary health centre analogous to the district general hospitals of the present time. These would in turn be linked to a teaching hospital, which would treat patients with more complex problems. The report expanded on these principles in some detail and the reader today would recognise many of the features that dominated health care in Britain through the second half of the last century. However the Council did not go into detail regarding payment for treatment regarding this as outside its immediate remit. Some members apparently considered that curative services at health centres should be free of charge to the individual patient. The possibility of partial payment based on insurance was considered and it was mentioned that contribution by the patient "could, as a rule, only be a contribution to the cost, for it has already been pointed out that efficient treatment will often be beyond the means of most citizens to provide in its entirety".

The paragraphs dealing with recuperative centres are of particular interest in relation to the Horder Centre. The Council clearly saw a need for such services, something which had almost certainly been brought to their attention by the thousands of injured soldiers returning from the trenches of northern France, many of whom were in desperate need of physical and psychological help. Recuperative centres were "intended to serve the double purpose of restoring patients to health either after illness or before their ill-health has become disease. A large number of patients attending doctors surgeries or out-patient departments of hospitals need rest, regime, fresh air, suitable food, physical training and recreation, to restore them to health and prevent the development of disease".

Paragraph 146 of their report describes how these services could be provided. "They need to be situated in the fresh air and require sufficient ground. They do not require elaborate buildings, and hutted camps offer many advantages; some of those still in existence might well be secured before they are broken up." After drawing attention to the wealth of experience available to the army medical service gained in the recent war they continued: "The experience of these camps also shows that the success of a recuperative centre would depend largely upon the possession by the staff of special aptitudes and training for this work". Although Bochenek saw her Centres as dealing with those suffering from a specific illness, rheumatoid arthritis, echoes from the past might well have resonated with her as she planned the future direction of her idea 30 years later after another devastating war.

Many of the changes proposed by Dawson, driven by the advances in medical science that were taking place, were far reaching and would take three-quarters of a century to develop. The costs in money and manpower caused by the Great War, the Great Depression of the 1930s and the Second World War meant that many of the ideas within the report, particularly those regarding improvements to the physical infrastructure, took many years to evolve. A detailed description of the situation in 1939 is given by Charles Webster in volume two of his authoritative analysis of the British National Health Service published in 1996.[2] In the public sector the Ministry of Health, through a Board of Control, administered general hospitals, mental hospitals and mental deficiency institutions, infectious diseases hospitals and tuberculosis (TB) sanatoria. Local authorities, through public assistance committees, ran the old poor law institutions providing 60 000 beds for chronic patients. There was a school medical service, run by local education authorities for the maintained schools and some of the private schools had their own small hospital to look after the pupils who were boarders. Small hospitals were run by local doctors working independently and national insurance committees directly responsible to the Ministry of

Health paid those doctors who looked after "panel patients". Maternity and domiciliary midwifery together with child welfare services had their own chain of command through statutory and non-statutory health committees to the local authorities and thus the Ministry.

Voluntary hospitals, which included the 24 undergraduate teaching hospitals, many of which were concentrated in London, provided 77 000 beds mainly providing acute services. The voluntary sector also provided home nursing care and there were societies for those who required after care following serious illness and other conditions such as TB, mental illness or mental handicap. Care of the elderly and chronically disabled, was often undertaken in nursing homes and in the absence of any therapeutic option treatment was confined mainly to the provision of good long-term nursing care.

James Le Fanu in his book *The Rise and Fall of Modern Medicine* provides a fascinating contrast between two men who he refers to as "two dominant figures of the pre-war years in Britain, Lord 'Tommy' Horder of London's St Bartholomew's Hospital and Sir Thomas Lewis of University College Hospital".[3] Lord Horder was a master clinician of the old school whose great skills were founded on making a diagnosis from the patient's history and observation of the physical signs found during examination, a system known as "clinical methods". Students who learnt the art of medicine in the first half of the twentieth century knew that a study of the textbook *Hutchison's Clinical Methods* was essential if they were to pass their examinations. As Le Fanu puts it "This was traditional doctoring, unencumbered by the trappings of technology, and its essential feature was the human relationship between doctor and patient". At the same time Sir Thomas Lewis was carrying out studies based on experimental work in his laboratory at on the heart rhythm using the newly invented electrocardiogram. This scientific approach to clinical medicine, which Lewis referred to as "clinical science", was not only new but gave rise to much controversy at the time, as Le Fanu describes. "The science in question was essentially the application of the methods of physiological investigation to man." It was to change fundamentally the way in which doctors practised medicine.

During the first half of the century the clinical methods practised by Horder led the way but whilst brilliant diagnosis often demonstrated what the patient suffered from, the means of treating disease were limited. The advances in medicine described by Dawson in his report referred in general to progress in surgery that had followed developments in anaesthesia and the antiseptic techniques pioneered by Lister in the previous century. Pharmacology had yet to enter the modern era and apart from exceptional breakthroughs by men such as Banting and Best with their discovery of insulin in Toronto in 1922, the therapeutic options available to the physician were constrained when compared with today. The discovery of penicillin by Alexander Fleming in 1928 and the introduction of antibiotics in the middle of the century changed all this and the clinical science of Lewis became increasingly important.

During the war many of the hospitals in London and other large cities had been damaged by German bombs and I recall the bomb site that still remained at the Westminster Bridge end of St Thomas' Hospital when I was a student there in the fifties.

King George V1 and Queen Elizabeth inspecting bomb damage at St Thomas's Hospital in September 1940 and the wreckage of the Treasurer's House. Courtesy of King's College Archives

When John Pullan, a former surgeon at St Thomas's, died in 1997 these times were referred to in his obituary. At the height of the Blitz when he was working as a young house surgeon at the hospital, he and his future wife, a nurse, decided to marry on an impulse having decided they were unlikely to survive the week. During the service a quantity of brick dust fell from the ear of the Chaplain for which he apologised having spent the previous night half buried under the ruins of his house. Further details of the damage caused to this hospital during the war have been described by Frank Cockett who became a consultant surgeon at the hospital and who was there as a young man during the war.[4]

Many of the nation's hospitals by the time the war ended were in a parlous state to say the least. The medical school at St Thomas's was bombed out in September 1940 and in 1941 a temporary hospital at Godalming in Surrey, known as St Thomas's Hydestyle was opened, to which the medical school and many of the medical staff and nurses moved. An anatomy unit was soon built and a medical library was opened in Guildford. St Thomas's staff also took over hospitals on the periphery of London at Woking, Botley Park, Brookwood and at Pyrford where an old TB Hospital became the Rowley Bristow Orthopaedic Hospital. Although the teaching hospitals remained in London, many established links with hospitals on the outskirts where the bombing was less severe. In most cases the buildings were of Edwardian or Victorian origin and some dated from even earlier times. The disruption of the acute hospitals and the post-war austerity which followed meant that providing facilities for the chronic sick and long-term disabled people was low on the list of priorities. It was to take the best part of half a century to re-furbish the NHS estate, something which finally began in earnest in 1962 with the introduction by Enoch Powell of his 10-year *Hospital Plan*.[5] Powell planned the closure by 1975 of 1250 small or specialist hospitals, a decision that often led to considerable controversy at the time. These hospitals would be replaced by 90 new district general hospitals at a cost of £500 million, the equivalent of £49 000million in 2012, with remodelling of 134 more. In the event it was to take far longer than 10 years for this re-building plan to be carried out.

The *National Health Service Act* of 1948 envisaged "a service comprehensive in scope, including medical and allied services of every kind".[6] This vision of the future is remarkably similar in principle to that of Dawson a quarter of a century before. However what was new was the concept, foreseen by some members of the earlier Consultative Council, that the service would be free at the point of delivery to the individual patient. Very soon it became clear that even this principle was to be severely tested by the forces of reality and the introduction of prescription charges three years after its inception which led to Bevan's resignation following the 1951 budget moderated even this ambitious aim. Financial control was to pass from the many different organisations that had previously been responsible for local services to the Treasury. The extraordinary concept often said to have been in the mind of Bevan when he drove his Act through Parliament, that as the health of the general population improved as a consequence of the universal availability of high-quality care the demand for it and thus its cost would fall, was shown to be fallacious. The rapid development of medical science began to place ever-increasing demands on the acute sector of the service and some things had to give as the Treasury tightened its grasp on NHS finances. Among the first services to give way, if they had been introduced at all, were those providing care for the elderly, the chronically sick and the mentally ill. In spite of the determined efforts of many well-meaning individuals and organisations over the years these services remain the Cinderella services to this day.

An interesting insight into the way in which the NHS authorities and the medical profession approached the problem of the chronically sick is

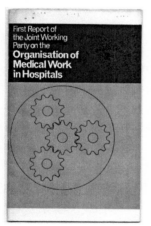

found in the *First Report of the Joint Working Party on the Organisation of Medical Work in Hospitals*, known as the *Cogwheel Report*, a pseudonym derived from its front cover, which was published in 1967.[7] This Working Party under the Chairmanship of the then Chief Medical Officer Sir George Godber was set up to "To consider what developments in the hospital service are desirable in order to promote improved efficiency in the organisation of medical work". Bed management was one of the problems it looked at.

"Some consultants, in order to prevent allocation of a bed to a patient with a chronic illness who might 'block' it for a long period, have adopted the practice of retaining a patient who could have been discharged, until the bed can be filled by a patient with an 'acute' illness. This misuse could be prevented by improved arrangements for transfer of patients with chronic illness and requiring the same facilities to other accommodation. While it is appreciated that the necessary accommodation is not available in all areas, improved bed management on a group basis and better liaison between hospitals and local authorities, such as could be achieved through an effective executive committee of the medical staff, could do much to improve the situation."

It was becoming clear that the outdated hospital buildings that the

NHS had inherited were, to use a current idiom, "not fit for purpose". At the time therefore that Cecilia Bochenek was about to open her new modern Centre at Crowborough to care for those who were chronically disabled by rheumatoid arthritis, the NHS was already finding it increasingly difficult to cope with the ever-increasing demands placed upon it by the chronically sick. A newly built establishment providing care and treatment for such patients in single-room accommodation in spacious grounds in the country, as envisaged by Dawson, was unusual at the time and remains so today. Those who were no longer considered to have an acute illness, were blocking the hospital system by occupying beds that were needed for patients with more acute illnesses who were presenting themselves in ever-increasing numbers. By discharging patients to establishments funded by local authorities or other organisations, it was hoped that the shortfall of beds caused by the presence of the chronically sick in NHS hospitals could be overcome and more acutely ill patients would be treated.

Bochenek had always intended that the patients who were admitted to the Horder Centre would be funded either by their local authorities or by the NHS. In October 1967, Peake had presented a report to the committee describing these arrangements. Since 1965 she had been negotiating with the South East Metropolitan Regional Hospital Board but had been unable to arrange a contract. The first patients had all, apart from two, been funded by the welfare departments of their local councils on the basis that they were in need of Part 3 accommodation under the National Assistance Act. Two patients who paid for themselves were charged £210* and £260 respectively, £210 being the maximum amount the councils would pay, which Peake pointed out "falls gravely short of the cost of maintaining and treating patients". However at the time of her report the situation had improved considerably. The Regional Board approached her and offered a contract to fund five beds on a regular basis at a cost of £320 a bed and from then on these beds were used to the full.

There is no doubt that at the time of her initial vision in 1952 Bochenek was taking a contrarian view in the light of what was happening at a national level in health care. At a time when the state had taken over the care of the sick,

---

* In Part 2 of this book, the monetary figures shown are, unless otherwise stated, those of costs updated as at 2012.

Bochenek was intending to set up an independent rehabilitation centre outside the confines of the state system. However she was also proposing to supply that service free at the time of admission to the patients in line with the philosophy recently introduced by Bevan. The Centre was neither a 'private' facility in the sense that patients would have to pay for their care, unless they chose to do so, nor was it part of the NHS. It was an independent organisation.

When Lord Horder encouraged Bochenek to carry on and develop her idea he probably had doubts that the proposed new health service would provide all that was required for those with advanced rheumatoid arthritis and other chronic illnesses and this indeed proved to be the case. It is unlikely that he would have encouraged her to set up an independent unit at that time had he not thought it would provide a service which the NHS would not or could not. By 1967 it seems the NHS was already beginning to be forced into using facilities outside the state service in order to cope with the increasing demands of acute medicine. The move to fund the five beds at the Centre by the South East Metropolitan Regional Hospital Board was at that time very far sighted and unusual and can be viewed as a pragmatic attempt to overcome a steadily increasing problem regarding the care of the chronically sick.

In 1982 another restructuring of the NHS took place with the abolition of the 90 Area Health Authorities and their replacement by 192 District Health Authorities. In February 1983 the Secretary of State for Health, Norman Fowler, announced that he was setting up an enquiry under the chairmanship of Roy Griffiths, to look into the effective use and management of manpower and related resources in the NHS.[8] Roy Griffiths, deputy chairman and managing director of Sainsbury's, headed a team of three other leading industrialists, one of whom, Sir Brian Bailey, chairman of Television South West, was also chairman of the Health Education Council and a former chairman of the South Western Regional Health Authority. By October that same year, demonstrating a speed of response unknown in the NHS both then and now, the *Griffiths Report* had been sent to the Minister and presented to Parliament.

Sir Roy, as he later became, and his small team examined the organisation and did not like what they found. They discovered a lack of a clearly defined general management function throughout the NHS and summarised their finding in what was to become a famous turn of phrase. "In short if Florence

Nightingale were carrying her lamp though the corridors of the NHS today she would certainly be searching for the people in charge." They defined their concept of general management as "the responsibility drawn together in one person, at different levels of the organisation, for planning, implementation and control of performance". At no level of the NHS at that time had they found it. They were not asked to concern themselves with matters that might be contracted to the private sector but suggested that "NHS management itself, however, should continually be asking how services are organised elsewhere; considering whether particular NHS functions could be performed to the same standard outside at less cost; and examining why, if functions can be performed more cheaply, the NHS itself should not do so".

It is interesting to compare these observations on NHS management with the early management style as seen in the early years of the Centre. There can be little doubt that if Florence Nightingale had appeared in the corridors of the Horder Centre in the 1970s she would have found out very quickly who was in charge. She would, it can be assumed as she was escorted around by Cecilia Bochenek, have been impressed by the new buildings that had sprung up as a result of the endeavours of a small band of dedicated individuals at a time when the health services of the country at large were still being made available in hospital buildings with which she would have been instantly familiar. She might have asked "why if this wonderful facility is available and the need is there is it not being used to its maximum capacity for the benefit of those in need?" Sir Roy, had he been asked to visit Crowborough in 1983, might well have asked the same question. He had ended his report with two sentences which are as pertinent in 2012 at a time when yet another in-depth review of the NHS has just taken place as they were in 1983:

"There have been over the years many working reports on, and much discussion about, many of the areas we have considered. The point is that action is now badly needed and the Health Service can ill afford to indulge in any lengthy self imposed Hamlet-like soliloquy as a precursor or alternative to the required action."

The Government responded by requiring Health Authorities to establish general management and find general managers to carry the programme forward as outlined in the report. In some areas this was indeed successful, in others it was not. The chairman of the NHS Management Board, Victor

Paige, who had been appointed in 1985, resigned after a year exasperated by political interventions and the failure in his view to appoint sufficient doctors and nurses to the new management structure. Where competent managers were found and appointed, opportunities to improve the service to patients evolved. The Horder Centre was fortunate in that it was situated in a Region where there were a number of senior managers who were aware, to quote from the Griffiths report that "the National Health Service is about delivering services to people. It is not about organising systems for their own sake". By taking advantage of this enlightened environment in its own Region it became possible to move the Centre forward into a new era.

The patients whom Bochenek aimed to help in her Centre were those who like herself had been diagnosed, no doubt by clinicians trained in the art of clinical methods, that little more could be done for them. The ravages of rheumatoid disease wreaked havoc on the patient's heart and joints and active treatment to prevent this was extremely limited. With the advances in clinical science in the realms of pharmacology, rheumatology and orthopaedic surgery in the second half of the century all this was to change. The patients of Bochenek's era would be replaced by those in need of, and indeed expecting, a different treatment regime and to meet the challenge the Horder Centre would also have to change its focus.

The NHS is often portrayed nowadays as a business with its income derived from taxation, providing a service to its customers 'free' at the time of delivery. As long ago as 1920, Dawson and his colleagues described the difference as they saw it between a commercial business and a medical service. A successful business receives its capital from its shareholders and its income from selling its products. The more successful it is the more money it makes and if it keeps its costs low and sells a product people want, it makes a profit and can develop the business further. A health care system of which the taxpayer is the shareholder and which produces a product the customer does not pay for survives by putting ever-increasing demands on the taxpayer and by running its affairs, it is hoped, more efficiently. The more successful the service becomes in terms of providing what its patients want the more unsustainable it becomes as its drain on the country's resources increases to unmanageable levels. The only way to reduce cost is to ration demand, so-called efficiency savings, and control quality neither of which is appreciated by the users. Any attempt to instigate such control immediately gives rise to howls of protest from its supporters, particularly those with entrenched interests, regardless of how rational these attempts may be. A monolithic state system with its inevitably politicised bureaucracy which stifles both enterprise and initiative is thus inevitably doomed to mediocrity. How to square that circle is something that has so far eluded academics, politicians and managers alike. As will be seen here a more locally based regional arrangement as suggested by Dawson, later adopted by Bevan and pursued in the early years of the NHS, albeit overseen from the centre, allowed the Horder Centre to change direction in the 1980s and pursue an individual path alongside, yet outside the state system. Such a structure where personal contact can flourish allowing individuals to reach their full potential in the presence of enlightened management would seem to be the best way to obtain the participation of pioneering individuals and professionals so essential to the success of any effective health care system.

Further Reading

1. Interim Report on the Future Provision of Medical and Allied Services. Dawson Report. Ministry of Health, London: HMSO Cmd 693; 1920.

2. The Health Services since the War. Volume 2. Government and Health Care. The British National Health Service 1958-1979 by Charles Webster. HMSO Stationery Office; 1996. Appx 2.1 p786.

3. The Rise and Fall of Modern Medicine by James Le Fanu. Part 1, 2 Clinical Science: A New Ideology for Medicine: London Abacus; 2011. p226-228.

4. The War Diary of St. Thomas's Hospital 1939-1945. Edited Frank & Dorothea Cockett. The Starling Press Ltd; 1991.

5. Like the Roman – The life of Enoch Powell by Simon Heffer. Weidenfeld & Nicholson; 1998. p290.

6. From Cradle to Grave. Fifty years of the NHS by Geoffrey Rivett. King's Fund Publishing; 1998. p30.

7. Organisation of Medical Work in Hospitals. Ministry of Health, London: HMSO 1967. para 45, p12.

8. NHS Management Inquiry: Griffiths Report. DHSS; 1983.

WHERE NOW?

The year 1981 was overshadowed throughout by the death of Cecilia Bochenek and the changes in management that followed. The chairman, Sir Derek Gilbey, and the committee had been struggling for some time to maintain momentum in the face of a decrease in the number of admissions. At the beginning of July only 21 of the 40 beds were occupied.

In January, Dr Jonathon Maw, who had joined the committee in 1973, wrote to the general manager of Nuffield Nursing Homes Trust (NNHT) in an attempt to attract a number of private referrals to supplement the declining income obtained from the National Health Service (NHS) and local authorities. This approach led to a visit to Crowborough by the Assistant General Manager of the trust who, whilst being impressed by the purpose-built facility, pointed out that it was often difficult to make full use of facilities that were relatively distant from main centres of population. He also stressed that patients' expectations were "becoming increasingly high on the standard of accommodation which they use". He thought "you may find it necessary to dress up the building in some way - to make it for example, nearer to the appearance of an NNHT hospital". There for a while the matter rested, although the door remained open for another approach.

In April 1981, Dorothy Beaumont was appointed administrator/ secretary to the Centre with a salary of £25 000 a year. Born in Yorkshire she had trained in business studies and then spent 14 years in commerce in Bradford before spending the next 9 years in Denmark in a scientific research establishment. This was followed by a further spell in commerce. She had joined the staff of the Centre in 1971, becoming a member of the Committee of Management in 1975. She had taken over much of Bochenek's work, in the year before her death, something which was recognised by the Committee who granted her a small honorarium when she took up her appointment in

1981. Construction of the new bungalow to which Peake would retire began shortly after this, Beaumont living in a flat at Clifford Court in Church Road, Crowborough, rather than in the bungalow Panorama.

One of Beaumont's first actions was to streamline the work in the office by introducing a computer system of which she had some knowledge. Although it was announced to the committee by Peake, who now that Bochenek had gone was seeking to take a firm hold of the management reins, it was clearly Beaumont's idea. Previously what she described "as a great deal of tedious checking" had been carried out by Bochenek personally. An anonymous donor had agreed to fund the cost of installing the necessary hardware and software, estimated to be in the region £21 000. It was intended to convert Bochenek's office into a computer room, which would also be paid for by the donor and at a meeting in April the Committee agreed to accept this offer with grateful thanks. Soon after, following the installation of a Commodore computer, a printer and a Wordcraft 80 word processing programme the Centre moved tentatively forward into the computer age.

At the same meeting when all this was discussed, Peake, who had long passed the age when she should have retired, said that she was prepared to carry on as Medical Director until such time as other arrangements were made. However, this drew attention to the need for long-term medical cover and at the next meeting in July, Sir Derek emphasised the need for time to be set aside very soon to discuss this and the future direction of the Centre. With this in mind, Dr Maw, who clearly understood the need for change, suggested that Mr Blackall, the company secretary of NNHT might be asked to visit, as his colleague had previously suggested, to undertake a survey on the question of need. This visit was duly arranged and took place in September, although it is clear that Peake was steadfastly opposed to this procedure. Indeed on the morning of the visit by Mr Blackall she wrote to the Vice-Chairman of the Centre, Cecil Baker, informing him "before this proposed 'shopping around' by Mr Blackall this afternoon, to let you know that I am herewith giving notice to end my appointment on or before March 31 1982".

Mr Blackall duly met Cecil Baker, Peake, Beaumont and the two doctors on the Committee, Maw and Wotjulewski. A number of interesting suggestions were put forward in his comments sent after the meeting, a copy of which, heavily annotated by Peake in red ink, survives. Peake's opposition to any suggestion that changes or new ideas might be introduced to increase the use of the Centre comes through loud and clear. Mr Blackall's summary suggestions that selected rheumatologists from different parts of the country might be asked to come to see the Centre or that visits be arranged by the British Rheumatism and Arthritis Association and the British Association for Rheumatology and Rehabilitation provoked a resounding rebuff. His suggestion that "a further area of interest concerning sporting injuries which would certainly bring in the younger patient" might be explored produced a veritable apoplectic burst of activity from the red pen. His final offer to come to a committee meeting to present his views and carry out a further survey if required was marked "No thank you".

However, the response of the Committee in November was very different. The meeting began with a proposal from Peake that following the very successful art exhibition at the Centre in October, art courses for disabled people should be set up and the 10 rooms in the new wing that had not been used so far should be allocated for this purpose. This idea was approved "in principle" but, perhaps fortunately, does not appear to have progressed further.

The Committee then went on to discuss Mr Blackall's ideas. Peake did not feel that "the report was any help to us at all and that she would be firmly against any proposal to proceed further. She was appalled at the thought of spending £2,100 on the suggested survey." Drs Maw and Wojtulewski and Mr Covell were of a different opinion. After a lengthy discussion and a vote it was decided to ask Mr Blackall to proceed. Dr Wojtulewski was asked to approach some of his colleagues and suggest a visit to the Centre and Dr Maw thought Dr Ivan Williams from Tunbridge Wells be asked "to be associated with us", an idea to which Peake objected. However, towards the end of the meeting it was decided that Mr Blackall be asked to carry out a survey to determine views and opinions of medical consultants, a local authority and organisations with an interest in arthritic care to help in forward thinking and planning. Finally Mr Covell put forward a suggestion that it would be advantageous if a person with more business experience was asked to join the Committee and he was asked to approach Mr Denys Milne, a former Managing Director of British Petroleum, who now lived nearby. This was to have far-reaching implications regarding the changes which were to take place later.

In January and February 1982 Mr Blackall presented his report in two parts. He had approached individuals and various organisations both here and overseas. The first part of the report dealt with the views of medical consultants and the second part with those of organisations providing care facilities for the arthritically disabled. Many of the consultants he approached were not aware of the Centre and as the distance from Crowborough increased so did the view that the distance reduced interest amongst patients. One doctor made the point that there was generally a lack of nurses trained specifically for the care of arthritic patients. Several consultants mentioned the need for hydrotherapy services.

A letter from the Jan Van Breeman Instituut in the Netherlands informed Mr Blackall that occupancy in rheumatology wards in specialist hospitals was steadily decreasing. If out-patient care was impossible, admission to the larger district hospitals where involvement of many specialists was available was now preferred. In the United States of America, his discussions with the Arthritis Foundation national office in Atlanta made it clear that because of cost shorter hospital stays were now recommended. It was increasingly difficult to get insurance companies or government agencies to pay for even short-stay care for people with arthritis and travel abroad for treatment or to a spa was increasingly seen as only for the very wealthy. An American clinician "made the point that it was time we took arthritis seriously since it was very much a neglected area compared with other specialties".

The report concluded that as in all forms of care patients liked to be in an establishment near their relatives. Increased costs "associated with the nation's general economic troubles mean less likelihood of NHS contractual beds between the State and private charitable and other nursing homes". There was a need for nurse training in the private health care sector with emphasis on care for people with arthritis. Blackall considered that the Centre would be ideal for this and might benefit from striking up dialogue with the private sector on the subject. He also found a widely held belief that to survive specialised units such as the Centre would have to diversify, possibly into the area of providing sheltered housing. Of particular interest however in view of the direction the Centre was to take a few years later was his view that "there would seem no point in adding an operating theatre and thus broadening into acute surgery". Although he did not mention it in his report such a move could have brought the Centre into competition with a Nuffield Hospital nearby in Tunbridge Wells, something he might well have wished to avoid.

At the same time that Gordon Blackall was producing his report, Dr Wojtulewski was arranging a visit to the Centre by two distinguished senior rheumatologists, Dr Rodney Grahame of Guy's Hospital, and Dr Bill Mace of Lewisham Hospital. They visited the Centre in January 1982 and put forward a number of recommendations having been asked to give advice on the future of the unit.

The visitors noted that at the time of their visit only 21 beds were occupied, with a maximum bed availability of 42. The public rooms and treatment areas they considered were grossly under used. They thought these areas would provide ample space "for those essential features currently not available, including occupational therapy and hydrotherapy". They also noted "Such physiotherapy as there is, is provided in the form of exercises performed to music advocated by Dr Peake. We saw no appliances for electrotherapy or ultrasound. There was no assessment unit for daily living activities".

Their report included a useful analysis of the Centre's financial position at the time. They were apparently informed that the current cost of maintaining a patient at the Centre was £640 a week and this cost was rising. From a funding point of view they divided the patients into four categories. Five beds were maintained in part by funding from Eastbourne Health District at a rate of £400 a week each, this being the payment agreed with the Region in earlier years. Ten to 12 patients were maintained by various local authorities who contributed £220 a week, this being supplemented by £74 from the patient. Some patients, presumably those who were not covered by local authority payments, contributed up to £260 a week, through various Department of Health and Social Security grants and allowances towards their upkeep. Finally the fourth group were private patients contributing up to £320 a week towards their care. It was assumed by the visitors that the balance of the cost was provided by the charity.

They also gave a brief summary of the annual accounts for the period 1972-1976, which it appeared were the most recent accounts to have been submitted to the Charity Commissioners. They found that the assets of the charity had remained at £6.9 million (updated for inflation at 2012). Income from local authority and NHS sources had totalled £1.3 million with an additional contribution of only £13 000 from private patients. Administration had cost £340 000 and the cost of running the Centre was £1.8 million.

Mace and Grahame concluded that the Centre had considerable potential as a major Centre for the treatment and rehabilitation of patients with severe physical disability, but they added a rider that "it is probable that most of the patients in this category now suffer from non-rheumatological disorders". They considered that its geographical isolation was a considerable disadvantage and that it was grossly under used. "In no sense can it be said to provide medical rehabilitation."

If the Centre was to survive they regarded it as essential that a new Medical Director be appointed at the earliest opportunity who was a doctor experienced in rheumatology and rehabilitation empowered to make fundamental changes to the facilities and the admission policies. Provision for hydrotherapy, "purposive occupational therapy" and updating of treatment areas was urgently needed. Once all this was completed consideration should be given to the long term. "Changes in medical and social practice may well mean that the need for medium or long term residential rehabilitation will change and this is particularly true of rheumatological problems." Bearing in mind the aspirations of the original founders they considered the enterprise to be a remarkable one but they believed that a major change in direction was now needed immediately if the Centre was to survive in "other than a very emasculated form".

These two reports came at a defining moment for the Committee. Until this point the organisation had been dominated by the authority of its founder leader and its direction had been guided by views that had led to a remarkable achievement but had been initiated to deal with the problems of a past era. Those who had now viewed it from an external perspective could see only too clearly that if it was to survive a radical change in thinking was required. Changes in medical practice had been profound and times of austerity meant that the ever-rising cost of health care had to be controlled, the easiest way being a reduction in residential care with a change to treatment in the patient's home whenever possible. This in turn meant an increase in facilities for treatment on an out-patient basis, recognised in the reports as a need for hydrotherapy treatment and the appointment of well-trained occupational therapists and physiotherapists. Most important of all was the requirement for an experienced clinician to take charge of the overall direction of the Centre and to take it forward in line with modern medical practice.

Had the Drs Grahame and Mace been provided with the latest income and expenditure account for 1981 they would have noted a rapidly approaching financial problem related to the increasing costs of running the Centre. Although income from charitable sources and patient payments had remained steady at £810 000 compared with the previous 12 months and the reserves had held up, the administration costs had almost doubled to £140 000 and the Centre expenses, which included medical and nursing salaries, had risen by £240 000, leaving a deficit for the year of almost £14 000 to be met from reserves compared with a surplus in 1980 of over £300 000. Clearly if this were to continue the future looked bleak.

In the first 9 months of 1982 the Committee met on four occasions. Much of the discussion focused on what might be called housekeeping matters but a number of important debates took place. The new bungalow was completed and Peake moved there in May having paid for most of the internal fittings and the landscaping of the gardens herself. Arrangements had been made as from the 1 July for patients to be transferred from her care to that of Dr Christopher Sampson, a partner at the local Beacon Road

Surgery, who would visit the Centre on Tuesday and Friday each week. Discussions took place regarding the possible construction of a hydrotherapy pool and in May an appeal was launched with the aim of raising £800 000 towards the cost. In that same month it was announced that Mr Denys Milne had agreed to join the Committee and at the July meeting he was welcomed by the Chairman Sir Derek Gilbey. Most importantly a short list of applicants for the post of Medical Director had been drawn up and interviews arranged, the panel to consist of the medical members on the committee and Dorothy Beaumont.

The next meeting was scheduled for October. In advance of that meeting Beaumont prepared a short document in which she outlined her thoughts on the future of the Centre. The impending retirement of the Chairman was noted and the recent appointment of Dr Douglas Woolf as Medical Director was announced. Beaumont considered that circumstances had provided an opportunity to evaluate the whole structure of the charity and lay a new foundation for the future. In putting forward her ideas for a new committee structure, which appears to have been a somewhat complicated proposal, she digressed to shed a little light on the problems she had experienced as Cecilia Bochenek's assistant. After outlining the debt of gratitude that was owed to Bochenek and Peake she went on "We also know that the very talents Cilla Bochenek developed in herself to such good effect were also the ones which almost destroyed the very thing she had worked so hard to build up. I hope there will always be people of quality associated with the Centre, and that they will be allowed scope to develop their talents, but it is equally necessary that there be an underlying structure which will function irrespective of personalities." In this paragraph Beaumont indeed exposed, perhaps inadvertently, possibly deliberately, a fault line that had run through the organisation since its inception as a degree of hubris increasingly influenced the actions of both Bochenek and Peake and they failed to comprehend the threats that lay ahead.

In the course of her report Beaumont announced that Dr Douglas Woolf would talk at the next meeting about the Centre, describing what he had found, his likes and dislikes and the way forward as he saw it. As indeed he did.

UNDER NEW MANAGEMENT

Douglas Langton Woolf, OBE, FRCP, DPhys Med, was born in London in 1919. The son of a general practitioner he trained at the London Hospital qualifying in 1945. After National Service he was duly appointed Consultant Physician in Rheumatology to Willesden Hospital and the Waltham Forest group of hospitals in 1952 and the Central Middlesex Hospital in 1975. He published widely and was active in numerous medical societies including the Hunterian Society, of which he was President in 1979. He edited the *Journal of Rheumatology and Rehabilitation* from 1968 to 1982 and was a trustee of Arthritis Care for 47 years, becoming its chairman from 1982 to 1988. A lifetime of service to Arthritis Care was recognised in 1993 when with Dr Barbara Ansell he received the Duke of Westminster award for professional service to people with arthritis. In 1998 he was awarded the OBE for services to Arthritis Care. He died suddenly in 2000 aged 81 years.

The Horder Centre was indeed fortunate to obtain his skills both in the professional and management fields. He served as Medical Director of the Centre from 1982 to 1989 until he retired aged 70 years and he was a driving force with regard to the introduction of surgery there. Following retirement he was appointed a Vice-President of the Centre. A family man with two children, one of whom, his son, became Consultant Rheumatologist for Cornwall and the Isles of Scilly, he had recently become a widower when he decided to take on the challenge at Crowborough. He was a tireless worker and consummate organiser and anyone who met him was at once struck by his warmth and charm.

He took up his post at the Centre on 1 September 1982. He very quickly assessed the problems and at the first meeting of the committee that he attended in early October he did not mince his words. The meeting had begun with a tribute to Cecil Baker, Vice-Chairman since 1976, who had recently died. Dr Peake's retirement was announced and her best wishes for the future were conveyed to the committee. She had informed the chairman that she would not be attending any more committee meetings. Douglas Woolf was then welcomed and invited to present his first report.

He began by telling the committee that he regarded his appointment as a challenge. "The Horder Centre had not been well thought of by the medical profession", but the fact that it had been built and had run for 16 years was in itself a great tribute to Cecilia Bochenek and Joyce Peake. He accepted that there were 22 people who regarded the Centre as their home. Seventeen beds remained, of which six were contracted to Eastbourne Health Authority and the question was how to fill these 17 beds. He wished to see them used by patients who would benefit from up-to-date methods of rehabilitation. However the presence of long-stay patients in wheelchairs was a problem and presented a very bad image of the Centre. Dr Barbara Ansell, a specialist with an international reputation in the treatment of children and young people with arthritis, had recently visited the Centre, no doubt on his invitation, and had felt it would be wrong for her to send young people to the Centre to be confronted by so many in wheelchairs. "Somehow we must create a new image as an 'ongoing Centre' instead of that of a nursing home filled by wheelchair bound patients." He wondered whether it would be possible to set aside one corridor for ambulant patients where wheelchairs would be banned from access although he accepted that this presented some logistical problems.

Dr Joyce Peake, Dr Douglas Woolf and Dorothy Beaumont in 1982

He and Dorothy Beaumont had started to hold regular meetings attended by staff representatives from all departments. A patients' representative had been asked to join and a useful exchange of ideas was taking place. A room on the lower level, which had kitchen facilities, was to be used as a recreation room for patients and the Charterhouse Trust had promised a grant of £9600 towards furnishing this room. An occupational therapist had been appointed on a part-time basis and would help Dorothy Beaumont with the furnishing of this room. He thought that 'Panorama', which was now empty, might be used as a Day Centre, although it would need refurbishment. He was writing to his colleagues to tell them of the facilities and was seeking sponsorship from pharmaceutical companies for meetings of doctors at the Centre. Syntex Pharmaceuticals had agreed to sponsor one meeting and Professor Eric Bywaters had been pleased to accept an invitation to give a Cecilia Bochenek Memorial Lecture on 19 April 1983.

A discussion followed regarding the hydrotherapy unit, which it was agreed provided an important means of treatment that the Centre would need to offer in the longer term. A feasibility study had suggested a cost of £1.1 million for the pool and ancillary services, which was considered to be too extravagant at that time. A more urgent matter was to upgrade the physiotherapy department and employ more physiotherapy and occupational therapy staff. It was decided that the hydrotherapy unit should be set aside for the time being and that the physiotherapy department be upgraded first.

The committee then discussed a memorandum put forward by Dorothy Beaumont regarding restructuring the charity. Ralph Covell, speaking for himself and Denys Milne who had sent apologies before the meeting, said that they would like to see the committee enlarged to widen the spectrum of available knowledge by incorporating, for example, bankers and solicitors. The members were not in agreement with her suggestion that the chairman should be a member of the medical profession. Douglas Woolf said that irrespective of any other changes he thought there should be a medical advisory committee. It was therefore agreed that the existing medical council of the Centre would be disbanded and the members asked as a matter of courtesy whether they wished to continue their association with the Centre by serving on the new medical advisory committee. It was also agreed "that Dr Woolf should invite Dr Barbara Ansell, Dr Colin Barnes, Dr Rodney Grahame, Dr Bill Mace and Dr Edward Huskisson to serve on the new committee". These eminent physicians were of course well known to the new Medical Director and by involving them, knowledge of the Centre and its activities would be spread far and wide in the profession amongst those who might refer patients, in a way that had not been the case in the past. Mr Derek Richards, the senior orthopaedic surgeon at Eastbourne was also invited to join this medical advisory committee, the first surgeon to become formally associated with the Centre.

At the first meeting of this medical advisory committee in January 1983 there was general agreement that a hydrotherapy pool was required and further enquiries with regard to cost were put in hand.

It was clear that "the winds of change" were now blowing through the Horder Centre. At a meeting in December 1982, Sir Derek Gilbey, who had already intimated that he wished to retire, confirmed his intention to do so and asked the committee members to elect his successor. As it turned out this was to be his last meeting as chairman. At the meeting of the committee on the 8 February 1983 he sent his apologies and "Mr Denys Milne was invited to act as chairman", which he accepted. He was formally confirmed as chairman of the Centre shortly after, at the Annual General Meeting (AGM) that took place on the 26 April 1983.

The arrival of Denys Gordon Milne to live nearby was indeed fortunate for the Centre. Born in the Shetland Isles in 1926, the son and grandson of

Denys Gordon Milne CBE
(Courtesy of Epsom
College Archives)

doctors, he was educated at Epsom College where he excelled at rugby and became head boy. A huge man at 6 foot 6 inches he was inevitably known as "Tiny". Before going up to Oxford University to read modern history at Brasenose, he served for 3 years in the Royal Air Force Volunteer Reserve as a pilot officer in the latter years of the war. He was a lacrosse and athletics Blue and represented Scotland in athletics. He served in the Colonial Administrative Service in Nigeria until 1955 before leaving to join British Petroleum in West Africa and then London, where he became Chief Executive of BP Oil Ltd., retiring

eventually in 1982 in which year he was appointed CBE. In retirement he became active in community affairs as a Director of Business in the

Community and a member of Eastbourne Health Authority. He was a trustee of the Centre for African Studies at York University and of the National Motor Museum. As a Member of the Court of the Worshipful Company of Carmen and a Liveryman of the Worshipful Company of Tallow Chandlers he maintained his contacts with the City and served on the Council of Epsom College as Chairman from 1990 to 1995. A superb raconteur, in retirement having been captain of the BP yacht club, he enjoyed sailing his sloop along the Dalmatian coast when on holiday or driving his vintage Lagonda or Bristol cars. He died suddenly in Crowborough aged 74 years on 9 February 2000.

The appointments of "Tiny" Milne as chairman and Douglas Woolf as Medical Director ensured the future of the Centre at a time when its survival was seriously at risk. Milne was a born leader with a style that engendered enthusiasm and loyalty amongst those who worked with him, and both men had entrepreneurial skills and energy, which they employed at a time when the Centre so needed their help. Most importantly they got on with each other extremely well.

In July 1982, just before Woolf took up his post, there were 33 patients in the Centre, many of whom were permanent residents. Bookings had been made for admissions in August, which it was hoped would bring the complement up to 39 and the Eastbourne Health Authority had just agreed to take on one more bed, bringing the total in the contract to six. An analysis of the figures is revealing. Of the 33 patients, nine were men, of whom five were permanent residents and two hoped to become so. Twenty-two patients overall were permanent residents. Twenty-six patients were over 60 years of age and of this group 14 were over 70 years of age. The Centre had clearly become a nursing home for the elderly, rather than a Centre for rehabilitation.

It was clear to the new Medical Director that this had to change. Kersley and Glyn, discussing the evolution of rehabilitation in their book *A Concise International History of Rheumatology and Rehabilitation*,[1] point out that the purpose of rehabilitation is to restore independence and dignity to disabled people. Although this had been the philosophy enunciated by Bochenek when she spoke of her aims in the 1950s it had not come to pass other than in a few isolated examples. To achieve this aim, the sooner evaluation starts following the onset of illness, the better. Writing in 1991, Kersley and Glyn quote as an example the United States of America, where the cost of an acute hospital bed was so much greater than in a rehabilitation unit. "As a result, rehabilitation in the USA tends to start at a significantly earlier stage than is possible within the limited resources for intensive treatment in the NHS."

The bed occupancy figures at that time demonstrate very clearly why Woolf stated at his first committee meeting that he regarded his post as a challenge. As a leading specialist in rehabilitation he was confronted by a group of permanent residents motoring around the corridors in what the lay public referred to as bath chairs most of whom were long past the stage where rehabilitation had a part to play in their life. Such 'treatment' as there was consisted of waving their arms about under supervision in time to music and rehabilitation in the sense of returning younger sick patients to the community to work, or at least to lead an independent life, was an illusion. In response to a comment from Richard Pace at the committee meeting in May 1983 that he was not clear about the aims of the Centre, Woolf explained that he was working towards developing the Centre as a rehabilitation unit to admit for a short term those who could be helped to maintain or regain a reasonable degree of mobility. The sight of severely crippled people with arthritis in wheelchairs could "have an adverse effect on patients who are less severely affected. This fact was preventing some doctors from recommending their patients to us". He accepted however "that a minimum of 10 long-term patients would be with us for a considerable time".

At the same time as Woolf was changing the medical policies, Milne was making changes to the Committee of Management and introducing new expertise. Ralph Covell, a retired architect and commissioner of taxes, became Vice-Chairman. Mary Carpenter, a former Director of Education at the Royal College of Nursing, Richard Pace, the current Director of Finance at Wealden District Council with wide experience in local government, Eric Panton, the senior partner of Gladstones, solicitors of Grays Inn and Clive Hearn, a chartered accountant in private practice, joined the three doctors, Maw, Steel and Wojtulewski already on the committee. It was clear that the Centre was open for business again.

Hearn soon expressed his concern about the large deficit disclosed in the 1982 accounts and the fact that capital was being used to pay current expenses. He had noted that the computer was under used and he was discussing with Beaumont setting up a payroll programme so that the finance officer could spend more time on other matters. In response to a question, Beaumont stated that to her knowledge no cash budget had ever been set up at the Centre. "It was agreed that this was essential."

In July 1983, Woolf again raised the question of hydrotherapy. When he had first come to the Centre there was a proposal before the committee to build a hydrotherapy unit, the cost of which he considered to be far too high when more pressing matters required attention first. However, he and the medical advisory committee as well as doctors who visited the Centre, were now of the opinion that hydrotherapy was essential if the Centre was to achieve its full potential. A decision was made to draw up preliminary plans and consult architects regarding the best site for the pool. These plans were presented at the September meeting and the suggested site, which was near to the water and heating plant room, meant that the original treatment staircase would need to be rebuilt, something that had been suggested before, so that the space it occupied could be put to better use. A number of donations had been received towards the cost of the scheme, an approximate estimate for which was £300 000. Hearn agreed that the use of reserves would be appropriate, although he would be worried if they were drawn on for running expenses. The Committee agreed that £260 000 be approved in principle and that item 6 on the schedule for landscaping and re-surfacing the car park at a cost of £44 000 should be set aside for the time being.

The first Cecilia Bochenek Memorial Lecture had been given by Professor Eric Bywaters on the 18 October 1983 before a large audience and Woolf said he was delighted with the outcome. He suggested that the next lecture should be planned for 1986, which would be the 20th anniversary of the opening of the Centre. Also that month the President, HRH Princess Margaret had visited and the members were very pleased to receive a letter from the Princess's personal secretary in which she stated how much the Princess had enjoyed the visit and the luncheon party.

Finance was still giving cause for concern at the end of the year. Hearn was expecting a deficit in 1984 of £380 000. He was of the opinion that all other money from investments, donations or legacies should be regarded as charity and budgeted accordingly. This should be available for development and additional works as required. As it was, the whole amount in 1984 would be needed to settle running costs. In discussion it was agreed that the need to subsidise patients from Eastbourne Health Authority and East Sussex County Council by the Centre was most unfair. After subsequent discussions between these authorities and Hearn, Eastbourne agreed to increase weekly payments from £390 to £490, leading to an increase over the full year of £29 000. East Sussex County Council also agreed to an increased figure of £310 for Part 3 accommodation that year.

A number of large donations were promised during 1983. A Miss Collis had visited the Centre and donated £87 000 towards the cost of the hydrotherapy unit, and together with other promised donations, a total of almost £100 000 towards the cost of the pool was now in the pipeline and architects were drawing up more detailed plans. However, unexpectedly in July, a letter was received informing the administrator that an anonymous donor had given the sum of nearly £0.5 million (£1.5 million in 2012) to the Centre. After arrangements had been made this sum was indeed transferred to the Centre's account at Barclays Bank from a leading Swiss bank. The Committee acknowledged the donor's wish to remain anonymous. Although not foreseen at the time, this gift to the charity was to play a major part in the establishment of the surgical unit in due course.

At the AGM in April 1984 the decision to proceed with the hydrotherapy unit was announced. The large anonymous donation was acknowledged as leading to a considerable strengthening of the balance sheet and the committee re-iterated its view that such receipts would be regarded as a bonus rather than planned income. The modest increases in the rates paid by Eastbourne Health Authority and East Sussex County Council towards the costs of the patients they sponsored were also reported. The Medical Director's report drew attention to the many improvements that had taken place regarding infrastructure and admission policies. However bed occupancy remained variable, partly as a result of financial stringency exacerbated by the Centre's distance from potential referring districts, which made it difficult for visitors of patients admitted on a short-term basis. The main aim now was to admit patients for further management of their arthritis and following orthopaedic surgery. To these groups were added those with neurological disorders and those requiring admission for respite care to help their families.

At the beginning of 1985, the committee was still struggling to find a way forward for the future. Hearn had presented his budget for 1985. The chairman commented that compared with the figures for 1984 the figures were similar and that they should prepare for a deficit of £520 000 for the year. There had been meetings with a professional fund raiser who had "stressed that neither he nor anyone else can be of any help to us until we know precisely what our aims are. That is something only we can decide". In February, Dr Malcolm Forsythe, the Regional Medical Officer, had visited the Centre again with a colleague but regretted that they were unable to recommend any means of funding the Centre. The possibility of taking in mentally or physically handicapped patients was suggested for whom funding was being allocated at £21 000 to £26 000 per annum for each patient. However the Regional Mental Health Co-ordinator advised that long-term placements would not be feasible although an occasional week to give carers a break might be possible. Dr Woolf was recommending that a few more elderly people with chronic arthritis might be taken to replace those who had died and after a long discussion at the March committee meeting regarding the future development of the Centre, when many avenues were explored, it was agreed that the proposal to offer six beds for patients with long-term chronic arthritis should go ahead. At the same meeting the final figure of £570 000 for the cost of the hydrotherapy unit was announced and after discussion it was agreed that the architects be instructed to draw up a contract with the proviso that everything possible should be done to avoid using the sum of £21 000 set aside for contingencies. After further negotiations a contract was finally signed with WH Price Construction Limited for work to start in November, with completion it was hoped by June 1986.

For some time Woolf had been pushing for an orthopaedic surgeon to be appointed to the committee. A number of patients were now being referred for treatment following hip replacement surgery and he was concerned that he did not have an orthopaedic surgeon he could turn to for advice. Derek Richards had been a member of the medical advisory committee for a while but Woolf now made a formal request that he be asked to join the committee of management. However there was a feeling that it was unlikely that Richards would have time to serve as he was heavily committed elsewhere. The chairman agreed but said "he would personally approach Mr Richards but had in mind the possibility of an honorary appointment rather than inviting him to be a full member of the committee". In September, Dr Wojtulewski, in support of Dr Woolf, pointed out that doctors had suggested that one of the ways of using the Centre would be to take orthopaedic patients rather than neurological ones and to have a surgeon actively involved. In addition it was noted that an orthopaedic ward at Tunbridge Wells might have to be closed in 1986, presumably to make financial savings, and there was a possibility that the Centre might be able to make its beds available to help out.

At the end of the last meeting of the year in November 1985 Milne said that "having got over the hump of the hydrotherapy pool, he would like to encourage members of the committee to think seriously about what the Horder Centre should be like in 1990 which is only five years into the future". In spite of the committee's best endeavours and much hard work, particularly by Douglas Woolf and Dorothy Beaumont, the Centre was still unable to find a secure role in the health care system where its full potential could be developed and its future ensured.

Further Reading

1. A Concise International History of Rheumatology and Rehabilitation by Kersley and Glyn. London: Royal Society of Medicine Services Ltd. 1991. p93-97.

THE PROLOGUE TO SURGERY

The introduction of surgery to the Centre owes more to serendipity than pre-arranged planning. In February 1985, as a member of the Council of the British Orthopaedic Association, I was asked by the President, Professor Robert Duthie, who had been the recent Chairman of a Government Working Party on orthopaedic waiting times, the report of which had been published in 1981, if I would be prepared to take part in a television programme which the BBC was planning called 'Doctors Dilemma'. They wished to discuss the problem of the long waiting time for hip replacement surgery, which was then fast becoming a national scandal. I agreed to do so and had the chance to meet John Yates, Research Fellow at the University of Birmingham who was on secondment to the National Health Service (NHS) and involved in a current Government initiative to reduce waiting lists.[1] In a discussion with him after the broadcast I said that I did not think that the NHS system of the time would ever produce a solution to the problem and neither of us felt the private sector had other than a minor part to play. It was necessary to develop a new initiative and he agreed to help, if I could come up with a firm proposal. He offered support from Government waiting list funds, of which he had control, providing that the Regional Health Authority would come up with a similar amount. We agreed to keep in touch and in due course when surgery was under way he visited the Centre. John Ball, who was to become the Centre's Chief Executive, recalls that he appeared to be impressed by what he saw and remained very supportive.

To test the concept that only by a new approach would it be possible to tackle this problem, I ran a small pilot project in my own unit at Hastings. With the support of the Chairman of the Health Authority, Rolf Killingbeck, and the District General Manager, Alan Martindale, I set up an arrangement whereby a hip replacement would be carried out in the operating theatre in the early morning before the day's routine work started. Clearly there would have been no point in doing this work during normal working hours as we would merely have displaced routine work and the emergency workload in the evenings was such that there was no time to feed elective surgery into the system. The staff members involved, apart from consultants, were paid a small bonus for turning up early. I promised the Chairman I would carry out an extra 40 hip replacements at a cost of £40 000 then and if we could do it for less I wanted to use any money left over to purchase word processors for the medical secretaries who were still struggling with old-fashioned typewriters. We carried out the task in record time and had £11 000 left over for office equipment. Clearly this way of dealing with the problem was unsustainable in the long term but the success of the experiment confirmed my view that only by adopting a radical new approach would the waiting list problem be resolved.

The support of my two senior management colleagues at local level was exceptional at the time as making money available to pay staff in this way was not within the normal financial parameters of the NHS. However it had meant that 40 patients who would otherwise still have been waiting to have their operations were now free of pain and the waiting list was that much shorter. I then recalled my visit to the Horder Centre in 1980 and the concept of setting up a surgical unit there where I could take patients from my long waiting list at Hastings began to take shape. I decided to approach an old friend.

Doctor, now Professor, Malcolm Forsythe and I had first met when we were working as young house officers at Lewisham Hospital in the 1960s. Our paths had diverged after that until we met up again when I returned to work in the South East Thames Region in 1980. I not only welcomed the renewal of an old friendship but also knew that he was, as Regional Medical Officer (RMO) of one of the largest Regions in the country, a leading figure in senior NHS management at that time. He was in a position to change things and I also knew him to be someone who could think outside the box. In November 1985 we met and briefly discussed the idea of using facilities at the Centre to carry out NHS work. I knew that what I was suggesting was unconventional but we agreed that I should take it further and that he would give it further thought. His encouragement and support at that moment was critical to the scheme's ultimate success.

Shortly after this I discussed my ideas with two colleagues, Derek

Richards, the senior orthopaedic surgeon at Eastbourne who was already on the Medical Advisory Committee of the Centre, and Peter Ring, my former senior colleague at Redhill Hospital where I had had sessions when I worked as a consultant at St George's Hospital in London. After our informal discussions they agreed to join me and we decided to approach the management of the Centre. Our initial approach was to Douglas Woolf, who kindly conducted two of us, Peter Ring and me, who were not familiar with the Centre's facilities, around the buildings. Following this we had a brief discussion with him about our proposal and he asked us to put our ideas in writing. It was agreed that I would do this and a paper signed by the three of us was submitted to the Centre.

Our proposal explained why we had approached the Centre at that time. The persistent inability of the NHS authorities to deal with the problem of the large number of patients urgently in need of joint replacement was acknowledged, a problem "particularly marked in the south east of England where there are large groups of elderly patients in the south coast towns which are principally retirement areas". In spite of the *Duthie Report*, widespread coverage in the media generally, including the television programme I had participated in, and continued pressure in the newspapers, "no real improvements had occurred".

However we noted a recent change in the political climate. The Secretary of State, Norman Fowler, in his annual report on the NHS, had commented that a reduction of NHS waiting lists could be achieved by sending more patients to private hospitals. The General Manager of the NHS, Victor Paige, speaking at the annual meeting of the Association of Independent Hospitals had stated "we must take every available opportunity to promote collaboration between the two" meaning between the NHS and private hospitals. We also drew attention to the fact that the NHS authorities were still talking about hip replacements seemingly unaware that "the development of knee replacement, of which one of us (SCG) has a particular interest, is developing rapidly". The South East Thames Regional Health Authority had estimated that the number of hip replacements in the Region would increase from 2188 in 1983 to 7600 in 1993.

We commented on the "modern purpose built buildings and magnificent site suitable for expansion. However we do not consider that the Centre can reach its full potential unless its present facilities are developed by building a surgical unit specifically designed for the treatment of the arthritic patient requiring joint replacement". We went on to outline our views as to how this might be achieved in the first instance by building "a single operating theatre with the capacity to expand to a twin unit. The provision of surgical beds is also required and we would envisage a standard 28 bed surgical block consisting of four six bedded bays together with four single rooms and appropriate nursing facilities". We also considered that for the plan to succeed it was "essential that the project be driven through whilst the political will is there".

In our conclusions we inadvertently echoed *The Dawson Report* of 1920 with our comment "Integration with the NHS is crucial as very few such patients [those requiring joint replacement] can contribute more than a little to their treatment from their own resources". Finally we set down what we considered to be the two crucial factors for the successful implementation of our plan.

(1) "The willingness of the NHS Authorities to support and use such a facility if it were to be developed. We believe that this support would be forthcoming.

(2) The willingness of the Chairman and Management of the Horder Centre to consider our proposals and carry forward the Centre establishing it as an international centre of excellence for the patient with arthritis thus enabling it to realise to the full the magnificent potential so brilliantly foreseen by its founders."

In January 1986, the Committee of Management met and a number of important matters were discussed, including the financial report for 1985. The Chairman was pleased to see that the charity receipts were well over budget, in particular from legacies. Unfortunately however expenditure over income was £570 000, £210 000 over budget. After a lengthy discussion it was decided that each department should be asked to reduce spending by at least 5 percent and that an overall saving of between £75 000 and £130 000 should be aimed for in 1986. Progress on the development of the hydrotherapy unit was noted and then the committee turned to the matter of future development.

Milne opened the discussion by stating that it was his idea that "we should develop our way out of trouble. A group of three orthopaedic specialists have enquired whether facilities could be made at the Horder Centre for the development of a surgical unit for joint replacement". The paper signed by the three surgeons was then placed before the committee. A number of members put forward their concerns and anxieties about the scheme and in due course Milne suggested that a sub-committee be formed to consider the matter and report back to the committee at the next meeting. He then invited a number of members to join the group, which he would lead, which in retrospect seems to have been composed of nearly the whole committee. He ended the meeting with a caveat that "if it was decided that a surgical unit was not a viable proposition we must find something else". It was clear that Milne knew that only a new initiative would ensure the survival of the Centre in the long term.

The Chairman quickly called the sub-committee together and in February laid his draft notes of the meeting before the full management committee and asked for comments. A long discussion followed with arguments for and against, including a comment from Milne, who was clearly enthusiastic about this new opportunity that had appeared on the horizon, "Crowborough cannot give us a living but the south east area can. If we were to become a place of national importance, Crowborough would wake up". It was eventually decided that Dr Woolf would contact the three surgeons enclosing a copy of the Chairman's notes from the sub-committee and ask for comments. Milne said he would like these comments in writing and it was agreed that until these were received no approach would be made to Dr Forsythe at Region.

Although no record of these comments from us remains, they were clearly encouraging and on the 26 April Woolf met Forsythe at regional headquarters. Apart from my earlier very informal approach to him the year before this was the first time the RMO had heard of the idea. Woolf took the opportunity to inform the committee in some detail of their meeting:

"Dr Forsythe said they were aiming to reduce the long waiting lists for orthopaedic surgery. South East Thames Regional Health (SETRHA) were now using Guy's and St Thomas' Hospitals for some of their orthopaedic operations. The Horder Centre should not feel themselves in competition with these facilities, but as a valuable adjunct within the area. In his opinion a twenty eight bed unit was quite unnecessary and we should use our existing short term beds - say nine or ten. He said we could forget about financial support from central government sources and that he did not envisage a centre of excellence. Dr Forsythe thought SETRHA would be prepared to consider funding 150 - 200 hip replacements per annum if carried out by surgeons in their region. They would not be able to pay for surgeons from any other region. He suggested that the Horder Centre submit a paper to SETRHA on the basis he had outlined and recommended that if we wished to take the matter further a letter be sent from our chairman to Sir Peter Baldwin chairman of SETRHA requesting a meeting."

Milne said that this varied so much from the original scheme put forward by the surgeons that before a meeting with Sir Peter Baldwin was arranged we must go back to the surgeons and "be assured that these surgeons were prepared to go along with the modified scheme". At the next meeting Woolf reported "He had had a further discussion with Charles Gallannaugh, orthopaedic surgeon, regarding the possibility of an orthopaedic unit at the Horder Centre". He described how they had visited rooms and discussed hiring a theatre unit to be situated off the Sembal lounge. A portable X-ray unit was considered adequate and medical cover provided by a resident house officer supported by a GP rota would be needed. Pathology costs still had to be obtained. A provisional estimate for charges was £1000 per week for rooms to which the cost of surgery needed to be added. Milne summarised with "our position has not changed. The scale has been significantly reduced which reduces our financial risk, but at the end of the day we have to be fully satisfied that we are covered by income".

At the meeting in September 1986, Derek Richards, who lived near the Centre, was co-opted on to the main committee. Woolf had been pushing to have an orthopaedic surgeon on the committee for some time to whom he could turn to for occasional advice, as a number of patients were now being referred to the Centre for rehabilitation following hip replacement surgery. Richards had been a member of the Medical Advisory Committee since 1983 and the developing surgical project meant that his presence on the Committee of Management would be particularly valuable. Milne announced that more detailed figures were available and a feasibility study had been prepared by "Mr John Ball, Director of the Sussex Private Clinic at St Leonards, who had been introduced to us by Mr Charles Gallannaugh". Milne had approached me earlier in the summer about the possibility of finding someone to manage the project and I had put him in touch with an old friend, John Ball. Milne had been impressed by the style of management at the clinic in St Leonards, which he had visited with Ralph Covell, Woolf and Beaumont. Figures presented by Ball, and adjusted by Covell to allow for additional costs, pointed to a capital cost of £750 000 to which needed to be added a cost for equipment of £280 000. Clive Hearn produced figures on the write-off of capital over time related to costs per operation and it was decided that 4 years would be the most practicable to take as a basis for negotiation. This showed an operating cost of £4000 per patient inclusive of a 10-day bed occupancy, which was normal for patients after hip replacement surgery at that time.

At the end of the meeting, Milne "recommended, and it was agreed, that a meeting be arranged with Dr Malcolm Forsythe, Regional Medical Officer, to seek his advice on the possible presentation of a scheme as outlined to Sir Peter Baldwin, chairman of the South East Thames Regional Health Authority". There was some urgency as Milne was leaving at the beginning of October for South Africa so he would make an appointment to see Forsythe for a short discussion as soon as possible. If necessary following this discussion a meeting of the committee would be called at short notice on 26 September, for as many members as possible to attend.

It did indeed become necessary to call a special meeting at which Milne reported on a meeting he and Covell, the Vice-Chairman, had had the previous day with Forsythe. The meeting had been scheduled to last half an hour but had extended to one and a half hours and the minutes record that "the Chairman felt there had been a very cordial response to the Horder Centre proposal which he had presented on the lines agreed at the meeting of the committee held on 12 September. Dr Forsythe had taken time to take the matter forward on his side on the assumption that we might be willing to proceed. Whilst speaking on behalf of the NHS it was obvious that Dr Forsythe had a good knowledge and understanding of the Horder Centre over the years. The atmosphere of the meeting had been such that the Chairman and Ralph Covell had not felt that they had been sitting on the opposite side of the table but had rather been participating in a round table discussion".

During the course of the discussion, Milne went on, which was at this stage exploratory prior to taking up Dr Forsythe's suggestion to make a formal presentation to Sir Peter Baldwin, "Dr Forsythe had explained that it would not be possible for them to regard a specialised surgical unit at the Horder Centre as a Regional service. This meant that the decision about the throughput of patients and availability of surgeons would rest with the Districts. He would therefore have to sell the idea in the first place to the District chairmen and general managers. He said there were many political problems within the NHS, the Region and the Districts, of which he had to take cognisance.

Dr Forsythe had asked, if it would be possible, assuming an agreement could be reached, for the surgical facility at the Horder Centre to be operational in the financial year 1988/89. It had been said that if early agreement could be reached this should be possible". However as events turned out this was not achieved and it was not until the following financial year that the surgical unit opened for the first operations.

At the end of a long but positive discussion Milne said that while the matter was being considered by the NHS, the Centre's management should be giving further thought to the housing of present facilities and changes to the command structure that the additional facilities would necessitate. It was then agreed that the Chairman would draft a letter to Sir Peter Baldwin requesting a meeting to discuss the proposal with him and send it to Dr Forsythe for his comments before submitting it directly to the Chairman of the Region. Milne was not a man to let the grass grow under his feet once the way forward was clear and before leaving for South Africa he composed a draft letter, which was sent to Dr Forsythe, who suggested that the regional manager should be involved at the time of the meeting. Comments had also been received from John Ball on the financial aspects, which Hearn had found "entirely acceptable". The letter was duly drawn up and signed on the 22 October by Beaumont as Chief Executive on behalf of the Chairman who by now was out of the country.

While all this had been going on, the hydrotherapy pool had been built. When the contract to build it had been signed in November 1985 a completion date had been set for June 1986.

There had been some controversy regarding the type of hoist for patients but this was soon resolved albeit with a small raid on the contingency fund that had been set aside. In committee Dr Wotjolewski pointed out "some doctors do not know much about the value of hydrotherapy" and it was suggested that it should be made the subject of an open day or seminar. For some time it had been the committee's intention to request that the President open the unit and negotiations took place with Her Royal Highness' secretary regarding a suitable date. It had always been intended that the pool would be in use for a few months before the official opening ceremony took place, which was eventually arranged for 11 December 1986.

The President, Her Royal Highness Princess Margaret, opening the hydrotherapy pool in December 1986. Dr Woolf and the superintendent physiotherapist, Mrs Rogers, are in attendance.

The pool building was duly completed on time in June and a very successful evening reception sponsored by Syntex Pharmaceuticals was organised by Douglas Woolf when it came into use, which was attended by approximately a hundred doctors and paramedics from a wide area. The committee agreed the initial charge for hydrotherapy would be £25 a session and in September Woolf reported that the service was much appreciated by patients and doctors. A new superintendent physiotherapist, Mrs Rogers, who had worked at Tunbridge Wells with Dr Ivan Williams who was now a member of the Medical Advisory Committee, had started in June and had been most helpful. A reception for physiotherapists was to be held in December and it had been decided to run a series of lunches to inform local GPs.

The year of 1986 had been a busy one for the management of the Centre. Dr Woolf had told the committee at the end of the year that at the Conservative Party conference that autumn, Norman Fowler the Secretary of State for Health and Social Services had said that he was hoping to be able to increase the number of hip replacements. It was an encouraging sign.

Further Reading

1. Why Are We Waiting? An Analysis of Hospital Waiting-lists by John Yates. Oxford University Press; 1987.

REACHING AGREEMENT

When Denys Milne wrote to Sir Peter Baldwin in October 1986, he provided him with a short, succinct summary of the present state of play as he saw it. He clearly wished to carry forward the discussion he had recently had with the Regional Medical Officer, Dr Forsythe, although there would be much debate following the proposed meeting between the two chairmen and their principal officers before a final decision was made. This important letter was to lead to the *Heads of Agreement* which took the project forward to fruition.

THE HORDER CENTRE FOR ARTHRITICS

CROWBOROUGH, EAST SUSSEX. TN6 1XP

TELEPHONE: CROWBOROUGH (08926) 65577

PRESIDENT: HER ROYAL HIGHNESS THE PRINCESS MARGARET, COUNTESS OF SNOWDON

REGISTERED AS A NATIONAL CHARITY UNDER THE CHARITIES ACT 1960 NO. 211622

DB/JEA/18550

22nd October 1986

Sir Peter Baldwin KCB
Chairman
South East Thames Regional Health Authority
Thrift House
Collington Avenue
Bexhill on Sea
TN39 3NQ

Dear Sir Peter

　　Our ideas for a Surgical Unit with 16 beds for hip and joint replacement at The Centre have reached the point where reference to you for agreement on underlying fundamentals is needed to enable us to go ahead with detailed planning.　Our meeting with the Regional Medical Officer was constructive and encouraging to the point where we have decided to carry our architectural planning a stage further for closer costing purposes but not yet as far as detailed drawings.

　　The principal question for us is a simple commercial one – the Charity is a small one and its reserves would be exhausted if we were to undertake this project and it would be irresponsible of the Management Committee to do so without specific undertakings as to the use of the new unit.　It is being planned as an adjunct to the public sector albeit in private (charitable) hands but being a Charity we must be open to all including private patients who will be welcome but who are not our primary objective.

143

Milne opened his letter by stating the case for the Centre, which was to obtain agreement to set up a unit of 16 beds for joint replacement surgery so that detailed planning could go ahead. The unit was being planned "as an adjunct to the public sector albeit in private (charitable) hands --- ". The aim was to reduce the backlog of National Health Service (NHS) cases to a tolerable level and the Centre needed to obtain a suitable long-term undertaking for the use of the unit it was going to build. The pricing philosophy was to have a break-even price "based on an annual throughput of 200 cases with a reduction in the price per patient if, as we very much hope, more than 200 are given". Milne was looking for an arrangement with regard to pricing that "would reflect not an arms' length relationship but a close association which, while leaving us masters in our own home, admitted you to the control of the budget". He then went on to give details of the cost per patient based on a 4-year agreement, which for 200 patients was estimated to be £4000. This would reduce on a sliding scale if more patients were treated, falling to £2100 per patient should the number rise to 500. However this did not at that stage represent the full cost as it did not take into account staffing the unit.

The recipient of this letter, Sir Peter Baldwin KCB, was a man known for his quiet reason and practical action and was exactly the sort of man

Milne was looking for to help him move the project on. Born in 1922 in London he attended the City of London School before going up to Oxford, taking a first in classics from Corpus Christi College. During the war he brought his formidable intellect to bear on the problem of decoding Japanese signals at Bletchley Park. He joined the Civil Service in due course serving as Principal Private Secretary to James Callaghan when he was Chancellor of the Exchequer and later as Permanent Secretary at the Department of Transport from 1976 until 1982, receiving his knighthood in 1977. On retirement from the Civil Service he was appointed Chairman of the South East Thames Regional Health Authority, where he was held in the highest esteem by his colleagues, and he also devoted his time to numerous charities concerned with helping disabled people. In an obituary following his death in May 2010 the writer observed that it was said of him that, if he had a failing, it was his inability when asked to help a faltering charity to say no.[1]

Sir Peter replied immediately to Milne after discussing the matter with his general manager, Peter Le Fleming and his colleagues. He added "we would like to follow it up with you to see whether we can arrive at an agreed basis for taking the proposals forward". Le Fleming was to meet the district general managers the following week and was then to get in touch to arrange a meeting with the Centre management.

When Milne returned from South Africa at the end of December he contacted Forsythe's office and asked for a meeting to be arranged as soon as possible. This took place at the Region's headquarters in Bexhill on the 26 February 1987 between Milne, Woolf, Beaumont and Hearn, on behalf of the Horder Centre and Forsythe, Le Fleming and Welling the Regional Finance Officer, for the Region. Unfortunately Sir Peter was unwell at that time and could not be present.

In March Milne reported on these discussions to his committee. He understood that Hastings was "in favour of sending orthopaedic patients to Crowborough but that Eastbourne had not made any commitment". Forsythe had suggested that Milne should meet Derek Platt, the Chairman of Eastbourne Health Authority, but although Milne had telephoned Platt he had still not been able to arrange a meeting. Forsythe had said that rather than wait for the *Heads of Agreement* to be settled he hoped that the Region could continue their internal negotiations whilst at the same time the Centre firmed up their plans and costs. In a letter at the beginning of April summarising his view of the meeting Forsythe wrote, "The Regional view as confirmed by the regional general manager, was that in principle we are very supportive of the venture to ensure an operating theatre and beds and the Region is willing to underwrite the equivalent of 200 operations a year for four years". He had met "the district general manager of Hastings Health Authority, Mr Martindale with Mr Gallannaugh and Dr Alexander, a consultant anaesthetist at Hastings, and Mr Martindale indicated that there would probably be support from the Hastings Health Authority but only on the basis of reimbursing the Region for around about £1,000 for each hip operation, this being the quote they feel they could obtain if they subcontracted the work to another NHS institution". Which NHS institution the district manager had in mind was not elaborated upon and begs the question as to why, if there was one, he had not used it already to reduce the very long wait for this type of surgery in Hastings. It is possible that he was basing this figure on the cost of the experiment we had conducted at Hastings before my first approach to Dr Forsythe. Forsythe was also pushing for the Centre to move things on by commissioning the theatre in January 1988 if possible so that advantage could be taken of waiting list funding available to Hastings in the current financial year as confirmed to him by the district manager following their meeting. In the event this did not happen but clearly the vibes were now right and the project was beginning to roll forward, although more slowly than some of the principal players might have wished.

Eastbourne remained reluctant to become involved and in a letter to Le Fleming at Region in July 1987 following a telephone discussion, Milne wrote that he was pleased "the Regional Health Authority's letter to us of 3 April holds good despite the discouraging muted response we received from the Eastbourne Health Authority". He also included details of new arrangements that the Centre had drawn up that showed the full cost with changes to the costs as originally proposed. The capital recovery factor over the 4-year period had been reduced from 100% to 50% and the capital cost provided by the Centre was set at £1.2 million with costs for staffing, services and equipment such as instruments and prostheses estimated at £890 000. The cost per operation therefore based here on a 14-day stay in hospital, somewhat longer than usual, was £4400 assuming 200 patients were admitted each year. He had reasonable expectations that this number could be increased to 300 in which case the cost would fall by £960 per patient. Forsythe responded by welcoming the updated proposals again pushing "to get the show on the road as soon as possible" suggesting that a temporary mobile operating theatre might be considered as it had "the advantage of speed".

In September 1987 the second Cecilia Bochenek Memorial Lecture had been given by Dr Frank Dudley Hart MD FRCP on the "Treatment of Arthritic Disorders since 1933" before a large audience. Tunbridge Wells had temporarily withdrawn support for its one contract bed and Dr Woolf was hoping to arrange with Arthritis Care for young people to take holidays at the Centre. The 'Great Storm' of the 16 October 1987 had caused extensive damage to the roof of the Centre and the doors of two patient's rooms had been ripped off. The electricity had been cut off for 30 hours although the emergency supply had coped and it was noted that the water tower had developed a slight list and a structural engineer was to examine it. The committee sent a note of thanks to staff which had helped in the aftermath of the storm. Unfortunately many members of staff living farther away were unable to get to the Centre the following day.

At the October meeting of the committee the Chairman announced that he had to report with regret that he had received a letter from Dorothy Beaumont indicating that she wished to retire when her contract expired in October 1988 and "It therefore follows that we shall need to find a replacement". During the course of this meeting in response to a question from Dr Maw as to when the surgeons could carry out operating sessions, "Mr Richards replied that he and Mr Gallannaugh already knew when they would be able to attend".

On the 8 December 1987 I attended a meeting of the committee together with my two colleagues Peter Ring and Derek Richards who was by now a co-opted member of the committee. Discussion was opened by Milne who said "we could not regard the assurances so far received from the Region as an adequate basis for spending a million pounds. He was by experience, cautious of any undertaking which was qualified by the phrase 'in principle' which was used by Dr Malcolm Forsythe in his letter 03.04.87. Discussion must continue until these words could be eliminated". I responded by saying "that from speaking to Dr Forsythe I was convinced the Region intended to underwrite two hundred operations per year and indeed, that they believed they had already given us a commitment to that effect". My colleagues agreed with me and we expressed the view that the only hope of improving the situation with regard to waiting time for orthopaedic surgery in the South East was to establish a specialised unit. Derek Richards added "The Horder Centre is being offered the opportunity to do this – if we do not accept someone else will. It could go to Midhurst, London or elsewhere".

Milne went on to say that the capital cost was not a problem but the operating costs for the basic 200 operations must be projected as accurately as possible and these must be confirmed as acceptable to the Region. "He believed that such a unit was a worthwhile project compatible with the ethics of the Horder Centre and one which would not prejudice the position of the long-term residents." It was then agreed that Milne would write to

Sir Peter Baldwin immediately to arrange a meeting. Subject to the full agreement of the committee and an acceptable undertaking by Sir Peter "the way would then be clear for the project to go ahead".

Sir Peter responded quickly in early January 1988 and in his letter gave Milne the assurance he wanted which Milne then read to his committee "I would like to confirm our agreement to underwrite 200 cases a year over a period of four years". A discussion followed and a consensus was reached that the Centre now had a firm enough basis on which to move forward. A formal exchange of letters would be made with the Region and it was agreed that when the Chairman wrote to Sir Peter he would send a personal letter to Dr Malcolm Forsythe. After this exchange of correspondence had taken place matters were put in hand to draw up the formal Heads of Agreement between the Horder Centre and the South East Thames Regional Health Authority.

What Baldwin and Forsythe had negotiated with Milne and his colleagues was quite remarkable in the context of that time and would still be very unusual even today. To use public funds to treat NHS patients in a hospital that was run and staffed by an independent operator was almost unknown at the time. They were putting their trust in the management of the Centre and the others involved to carry out their side of the bargain as indeed Sir Peter recognised in his letter to Denys Milne. He wrote: "From our point of view we are anxious that this proposal should make progress because this year and next year there is money to help us and our districts in meeting the costs of the 200 cases a year. After this the availability of special funds is unclear, though we will still have the commitment to pay for the cases". Milne responded with "We are as enthusiastic about this project as I know are members of your own staff and we shall do everything possible to bring it on stream as quickly as possible". The two chairmen had established an environment of mutual trust and no one involved in the enterprise had the slightest intention of allowing it to fail.

At the Annual General Meeting (AGM) in 1987 Milne had informed members that having completed the hydrotherapy pool the management was now "considering a serious major project which would take us on a new path, that of joint replacement surgery", although at that time he had given the chances of success as no more than 50 percent. However at the AGM in April 1988 that covered the events of the previous year, Milne and Beaumont were now able to announce "that a working basis had been agreed with the South East Regional Hospital Board [sic] about NHS patients being admitted for hip replacement surgery and other procedures". The Centre was to build an operating theatre and wards and the capital costs would be borne by the charity, the cost of an operation for a NHS patient being covered by the health authority. It was acknowledged that whilst the Centre could call upon its reserves for the initial stages it was essential that this depletion of reserves was made up and to this end a major appeal would be launched. The balance sheet for 1987 showed that the reserves stood at just over £2.1 million (£5.2 million today) at the end of the year.

In his report the Medical Director announced an increase in admissions on both a long- and short-term basis but regretted that many requests had to be refused because funds were not available in spite of the Centre's heavy subsidy. Referrals from orthopaedic surgeons of patients after surgery both locally and from farther afield now occurred and the major insurance companies recognised the Centre for private admissions. A close working relationship had been established with the rheumatologists nearby and he acknowledged in particular Dr Wojtulewski at Eastbourne and Dr Ivan Williams of Tunbridge Wells. The Centre was now becoming recognised more widely as a unit providing a modern rehabilitation service and was ready to launch into a new era.

Having now reached agreement to go ahead with the development of the surgical unit there was now an urgent requirement to appoint someone with the knowledge and experience to develop the project on behalf of the Centre. John Ball, the Managing Director of the Sussex Private Clinic at St Leonards on Sea had met Milne the previous year and agreed to assist in the early design stage. In March 1988 Milne and Covell had visited John Ball at his home to discuss two schemes that had been drawn up and submitted to the Centre. Ball had advised that the scheme submitted by Medical Installations Limited should form a basis for reaching agreement and had submitted 18 points of constructive criticism to be used in the negotiations. At a meeting of the committee in March discussion took place with regard to the role he should fulfil in the overall scheme of things. Some members "saw him as an advisor to our (building) sub-committee but others envisaged him as a 'supremo'". Dr Woolf felt very strongly that he should be regarded as a 'supremo' and said he had full confidence in Ball's ability to fill the role. Beaumont and Richard Pace felt likewise and Covell said he would like to see

Ball given clearly defined responsibilities of executive authority to speed up the project. The committee then agreed "that Mr John Ball be offered an ad hoc position of executive responsibility in respect of the orthopaedic project and be authorised to take such initiative as appeared desirable relative to planning and building, staffing and equipment". He would be expected to liaise with Covell, the retired architect, on architectural matters and Dr Woolf on all medical matters. Barbara Slattery, Beaumont's deputy, would act as coordinator between the practical development and the fund raising campaign, which would be running concurrently. The committee finally gave the Chairman authority to negotiate terms with John Ball.

While all this activity had been going on problems had arisen with the hydrotherapy pool. Just as Dr Woolf was increasing the rate of referral to the Centre for in-patient treatment from 112 in 1986 to 150 in 1987 with out-patient numbers also increasing, problems arose with the tiles on the new pool. A firm of architectural consultants was asked to give advice on the matter and concluded that the wrong type of tile had been employed in the construction and that remedial work was required. This would take 4 months to carry out and if further faults were found when the tiles were removed, 6 months, during which time the pool would be out of commission. The estimated cost for this work was £55 000 with a proviso that if other faults were discovered the cost would be higher.

The committee considered the possibility of setting up a temporary replacement pool while the work was done but after enquiry it became clear that this idea was impractical. Dr Woolf therefore suggested the Centre should endeavour to hire the services of a pool at Burrswood, a private clinic nearby, which they had done before whilst waiting for the pool to be built. In the event work to remedy the defects in the Centre's pool began in December 1988 and after a number of difficulties, such as the discovery of asbestos lagging in the original plant room, which had to be removed, the refurbishment was completed and the pool re-opened on 26 April 1989. In due course legal advice was taken and a writ for negligence was issued against the original architects.

Further Reading

1. Sir Peter Baldwin. Obituary. *The Guardian*: 8 June 2010.

CREATING AND STAFFING
THE SURGICAL UNIT

At a committee meeting in June 1988 a decision was made to offer the post of Chief Executive of the Centre to John Ball. The offer was accepted and in July Milne told the committee "that he thought it appropriate that he be invited to be in attendance at any meetings of the management committee held prior to his taking up the post". Dorothy Beaumont retired following the meeting on 28 September when the members paid tribute to her 17 years of service and presented her with a gift as a token of their personal appreciation. After due formalities had taken place John Ball took over as Chief Executive.

John Ball's early career had fitted him well for the task ahead. After a short spell of military service he had trained in nursing and after 2 years he left to work for Pfizer Ltd. as a sales representative. In due course he took up a position as a senior medical representative for Armour Pharmaceuticals based in Eastbourne, rising through the company ranks to head office, becoming eventually the marketing manager for the UK and Europe. I had

got to know John when I arrived at Hastings in 1980. He was then Chief Executive of the Sussex Private Clinic at St Leonards on Sea where in 1976 he had been a key figure in setting up a surgical facility where a considerable amount of surgery including joint replacement surgery had been carried out. We had become good friends and when I introduced him to Denys Milne in 1986 I was aware that he was looking for a new challenge where his entrepreneurial skills could once more be fully exercised. A man with formidable energy he had both the experience and knowledge that Milne was looking for to guide the project forward and I had formed the view that they were two people who would get on well together which indeed they did.

At the first meeting he attended as Chief Executive he proposed that I should be co-opted onto the Committee of Management. The Chairman acknowledged that the number on the committee might need to be increased particularly if people with specialised knowledge were required. He took the opportunity to remind members that "the committee of management are policy and decision makers and we seek only advice from the medical advisory committee". In April 1989 Derek Richards and I were elected, on the chairman's advice, as full members of the committee and we agreed to attend future management meetings subject to the demands of other commitments.

John Ball did not delay before building started as he waited for the bureaucratic machinery of the NHS to grind forward with the process of drawing up the necessary agreement between the Centre and the Regional Health Authority. In January, as building got under way, various administrative obstacles appeared with regard to drafting the *Heads of Agreement*. The solicitors acting for the Centre were having difficulty in obtaining any response to their enquiries when they contacted the Region. Region had mislaid the papers before discovering they had been sent to Eastbourne as problems had arisen when it was discovered that the Horder Centre was classified as a nursing home. This meant that all the papers had to be sent to Eastbourne District Health Authority, the supervising authority for nursing homes in the area. Further delays then occurred for which Eastbourne duly apologised to the Region. Clearly the usual arrangements for preventing any disturbance of the normal tranquil waters of the NHS status quo were working well. In the midst of this Feydeau farce the two chairmen, metaphorically speaking raised their bowler hats to each other, when Denys Milne wrote to Sir Peter Baldwin reassuring him "that the contractors are confident that that they will be able to hand over the theatre and related facilities in September". He looked forward to welcoming Sir Peter as an honoured guest at the opening ceremony to be conducted by HRH Princess Margaret in due course. In his reply Sir Peter was "pleased to know that the project was progressing well" and confirmed that he would be delighted to attend the opening ceremony. As far as the two chairmen were concerned the project would come to pass as they intended.

After a meeting in February 1989 between senior officers at the Region and the district managers of Eastbourne and Hastings matters were moved forward by Dr Forsythe. In a letter to John Ball having "noted that the process had become protracted" because "the heads of agreement is very much more detailed than I had envisaged and I would hope we could develop a simpler form of agreement with you", he despatched a senior member of his planning team to the Centre "to clear some of the issues". The formalities then began to make progress although it was not until September, just before the first operations took place, that final agreement was signed and sealed.

In January 1989 political developments had again moved in the Centre's favour. The Secretary of State for Health, Kenneth Clarke, published his White Paper, *Working for Patients*.[1] The principal idea was to free hospitals from centralised control by establishing an internal market in the hope that, by competing for patients, they would improve their standards and quality of care and thus attract more patients. However the key provision from the point of view of the Centre was a proposal that allowed the larger GP practices to apply for their own budgets whereby they could purchase a range of hospital services, mainly elective operations such as joint replacement surgery. This concept, to become known as GP fund holding, was an enlightened approach which led to major improvements in the provision of NHS services before it was abolished, mainly it seems for ideological reasons, by the incoming Labour administration in 1997. This action, in the opinion of the author, was possibly one of the most destructive examples of political vandalism in the history of the NHS, and one which was to have far-reaching detrimental consequences over the next 20 years.

In November 1988 tenders had been invited for the building of the operating theatre and surgical ward from three companies, two of whom responded by the deadline of the 19 December. After appraisal a contract was agreed in principle with Medical Installations Limited although it was felt that savings could be made without detracting from the smooth running of the project and without losing the quality that was required. On 10 January 1989 a letter of intent to confirm payment for preliminary work carried out prior to a formal contract was sent out, with work to start on ground works and drains immediately. John Ball agreed to take on the additional responsibility of clerk of works and the anticipated handover date was to be 31 August 1989.

The plan for the new surgical unit involved major changes to the old buildings with the operating theatre being built as an extension at the north-west end of the of the original physiotherapy block. This meant that a new physiotherapy unit would be required and the old unit would be converted into two 10-bed wards. The first plans submitted by the contractors envisaged a new lift and a new roadway. However to reduce costs it was decided to make use of an existing lift housed on the lower level near the hydrotherapy department and to reduce the length of the proposed new roadway. A model was commissioned to show these changes and was presented to the committee by John Ball in February 1989. At the suggestion of the chairman it was agreed that a plaque should be placed on the model in commemoration of the Vice-Chairman, Ralph Covell FRIBA, who had died suddenly in December 1988, and who had worked so hard in many ways to help develop the project.

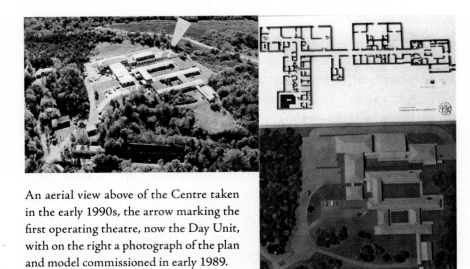

An aerial view above of the Centre taken in the early 1990s, the arrow marking the first operating theatre, now the Day Unit, with on the right a photograph of the plan and model commissioned in early 1989.

The model and plan of the site shows the operating theatre at the top right attached by a short corridor to what was to become the ward block. To the left of the wards separated by another corridor and a narrow courtyard were the new physiotherapy and occupational therapy units. The proposed new roadway, to be modified, runs along the top of the model curving round to the right of the theatre. The model includes the ward blocks and at the bottom the road to "Peake's Patch" completed in 1982.

Fund raising began in earnest again, led by the Chief Executive and the Centre manager Barbara Slattery. Dr Woolf organised a fashion show with contacts in London and a meeting at the Royal Society of Medicine attended by him and Denys Milne led to several eminent people pledging support. Professional fund raisers were approached but when little practical benefit followed as a result of this their services were terminated. The footings of the new operating theatre had been completed by the end of January but building was then held up by a national shortage of bricks until the end of February when bricks and bricklayers once more became available. Work started on the occupational therapy and physiotherapy areas with the aim of having these services in their new positions within a month, work going on in the evenings and weekends as required. Once these new facilities had been completed and the staff transferred it was planned that the builders would enter the old physiotherapy department to start constructing the surgical wards.

Mens tournament winner, Peter Thomas, receives his prize from Malcolm Forsythe.

Ladies winner, Brenda Brown, Theatre Nurse with Malcolm Forsythe.

At this time a League of Friends was established by John Ball and Barbara Slattery. A meeting in February 1989, which had been arranged to assess interest, had been attended by over a 100 people and a similar number who could not get to the meeting had written expressing support. Formal rules had been drawn up by the Centre's solicitors and when put to the audience the motion that a League of Friends be formed was approved. In due course arrangements were made to allow members to visit residents on a regular basis and organise outings, in-house entertainment and craft fairs. An important part of the Centre's integration with the community nearby, the members of the league were and remain staunch supporters of the Centre. Over the years the title has changed to that of Volunteers or Supporters, a process of evolution that maintains the ethos and indeed extends that of the original League. Early on, members helped to organise the "Hippie Walks" when former patients walked for charity in support of the Centre. A golf tournament between staff and former patients, first organised in the 1990s, continues until the present day with a band of enthusiastic supporters. The winners of the Millennium year tournament are seen on the left receiving their prizes from the then Chairman a regular participant himself. Today's volunteers help staff the new coffee shop and continue to assist with organising day trips and events. Through the generosity of local residents activities have been arranged within the Crowborough community helping the Centre to raise funds to improve patient services. In August 2000 a long-term volunteer Margaret Madgwick, who had had a hip replaced at the Centre in May, opened her own garden to raise funds and is seen in the picture arranging the raffle prizes.

In May 2012 a similar party was arranged by Mr and Mrs Kay in their own garden thus continuing the tradition of community involvement as so many others have done over the years. In 1992 a group of former surgical patients formed a Gardeners Club and assisted in planting a new garden area outside the surgical wing. In 1996 the first Therapy Garden was developed and more recently new therapy gardens have been built in the original courtyards between the wards with volunteers helping to maintain these. This help from local volunteers is an integral part of the Centre's activity today.

By April 1989 the need to employ staff for the new unit became necessary. John Ball and I had discussed the possibility of approaching a senior orthopaedic nursing officer, Mrs Lene Gurney RGN Dip Ed, who in the past had worked as my ward sister at Hastings before going on to an academic post at Hastings College training nurses to teach. Through our enquiries we understood that she wished to return to front-line nursing and as we had hoped, when she was approached she accepted the post of Senior Nursing Officer at the Centre from 1 June 1989 when she began work on setting up the surgical wing. She remained at the Centre as the Senior Nursing Officer until 2007 and continues to support the Centre on a part-time consultancy basis. Recruitment of a number of other surgically trained nurses took place and we were fortunate to be able to appoint Mrs Carole Otway who lived very near the Centre, as Theatre Superintendent. She had worked at the Centre since the 1970s initially on night duty. Starting with nothing she built up the theatre suite and a superb team of skilled theatre nurses and her calm but firm style of management was a key factor in the smooth running of the unit. She was soon joined by another experienced nurse, Mrs Katherine Ruck, wife of Dr Colin Ruck, the senior partner of the Beacon Road GP practice, which had been very supportive of the Centre for many years. To assist recruitment, in June a regional meeting of the Royal College of Nursing, which Dr Wojtulewski and I both addressed, was held at the Centre and according to the Chief Executive "we entertained forty plus senior nursing personnel from a very wide area".

Arrangements were put in hand to set up the post of resident surgical officer and the old bungalow, Panorama, was re-furbished for use as accommodation. The resident doctor would be supported by doctors from the Beacon Road practice who, with the agreement of Dr Ruck, agreed to cover for the resident when he was off duty and carry out ward rounds on Saturdays and Sundays on alternate weekends. In particular one of the partners, Dr Christopher Sampson, had stated that he would be pleased to be involved on the orthopaedic side and took great interest in the surgical activity. Dr Colin Alexander FFARCS, a consultant anaesthetist who had worked with me since our arrival together at Hastings had agreed to join me in the enterprise and under his guidance and with the support of a number of his colleagues an efficient anaesthetic service was soon equipped and established. Dr Jancis MacDonald, an anaesthetist from Eastbourne, worked with Derek Richards and Dr Tom Price, from the Beacon Road practice, who had a special interest in anaesthetics joined the team in due course.

Not all was smooth sailing. On 5 March 1989 the Kent and Sussex Courier had published an article describing the new surgical unit. In April a reporter from the newspaper contacted John Ball asking him to comment on criticisms of the Centre that had been made at a recent meeting of the

Tunbridge Wells Health Authority whose members were concerned over loss of staff. He had responded by stating that senior appointments had been made but not of staff from Tunbridge Wells. Soon after this, his response was reported accurately in a follow-up article in the newspaper and the committee at its meeting in May agreed that no further action was needed. However in April, Ken Tuson FRCS, a consultant orthopaedic surgeon from Tunbridge Wells, visited the Centre and made a tour of the building with John Ball and Dr Woolf and expressed some concerns. Following this meeting he was invited to attend the next committee meeting, which he did on the 18 May.

At the meeting, discussion started with John Ball giving a short summary of the nurse staffing situation. At that time a senior nurse manager had been appointed and applications had been received for the theatre manager's post and from four other RGNs and two enrolled nurses. None of these applicants were associated with the Tunbridge Wells health district. In May, two open days had been arranged for all grades of nurses which had been attended by a number of RGNs who were keen to start work and were particularly interested in the crèche facilities that the Centre was in the process of developing by converting the gatehouse. The chairman then invited comments from Mr Tuson.

Ken Tuson began by saying that "he came as chairman of the orthopaedic committee" (of Tunbridge Wells). "He said also that the article in the press had not come from that committee. The orthopaedic surgeons were not against the development." He then went on to outline a number of perceived threats and "said that the orthopaedic section ran on a shoe string". He ended his comments with "there was no antagonism, just anxiety". One of the perceived threats apparently put forward by the clinicians at Tunbridge Wells was that the development would have a detrimental effect on the Intensive Treatment Unit (ITU) thereby requiring the transfer of patients to the unit should the need arise following surgery. At a subsequent meeting between the chairman of the Tunbridge Wells medical executive committee and the Regional Medical Officer, Dr Forsythe indicated that the effect would be no different to that from the local private hospitals. Nothing more was heard of the matter.

After discussion in which the committee members did their best to reassure him, in particular concerning his and his colleagues' anxiety that the project would increase financial pressures on Tunbridge Wells, Milne asked Tuson "to take back the message that the Horder Centre had been given a sum of money and felt the project was a good way of using it". Ken Tuson thanked the committee and left the meeting.

Among other matters discussed at this meeting in May was the question of providing instruments for the operating theatre. Derek Richards and I had introduced John Ball to the chairman of Howmedica UK, a leading manufacturing company of prostheses and surgical instruments at the time and it had been agreed that the company would provide the instruments required free of cost to the Centre. However in due course it became clear that this, not unreasonably, only applied to specialist instruments as required for joint replacement surgery so the general surgical instruments would have to be purchased. As a result of this misunderstanding some time had been lost and although the ingenuity of the Chief Executive had led to the acquisition of much that was required some items were still outstanding. Fortunately arrangements were made to borrow such equipment for the first operating session. In 1998 Howmedica was acquired from Pfizer by Stryker which thereby nearly doubled its size with worldwide sales in 2004 reaching 4.3 billion dollars. Stryker have continued to be generous supporters of the Centre and in 2006 contributed the major part of the cost for the conversion of the first operating theatre, which was converted into a new state-of-the-art theatre and endoscopy suite, increasing the Centre's operating capacity and thus helping reduce waiting times. The support provided by industry, and Stryker in particular, is a vital factor in the constant drive to improve and extend a high-quality service to more patients, which the Centre endeavours to achieve.

The hydrotherapy department had re-opened in April 1989 and John Ball reported that the new physiotherapy department would open in May as would the new occupational therapy unit. Dr Woolf's retirement was now imminent and the need to find someone to replace him was becoming urgent. The Chairman announced that it had been decided to retain the title of Medical Director and the person appointed should be a rheumatologist. The Medical Advisory Committee had been asked for advice and had put forward the name of Dr Ivan Williams for the appointment. It was decided that "the chairman will meet Dr Williams in the near future". Shortly afterwards Dr Williams took over from Dr Woolf.

Dr Ivan A Williams FRCP DPhys Med, was the consultant

rheumatologist at Tunbridge Wells. A senior rheumatologist with a national reputation based on his large practice in Tunbridge Wells, he took over from Douglas Woolf in August 1989 shortly before the new surgical unit was opened. The introduction of surgery would lead to a very different

situation with regard to the care of the patients in the Centre, which was about to change from a rehabilitation centre with a number of long-term residential patients, into a hospital. His whole-hearted support for the project and his outstanding clinical skills were of critical importance in the provision of a safe clinical environment for patients. He and I had worked together for a number of years running a combined clinic at Hastings attended by patients with rheumatoid arthritis drawn from our respective practices at Hastings and Tunbridge Wells and I could not have hoped for anyone better to take over at this critical time. I was delighted when he accepted the post of Medical Director.

The last meeting of the committee before the start of surgery took place on the 7 September. Dr Williams drew attention to the fact that "there was a general lack of knowledge that the Horder Centre exists". A good deal of discussion then took place with regard to publicising its activities during which John Ball informed members of three open days that had been arranged in September for local civic leaders, doctors and local people. He had written to all medical insurance companies informing them of the inaugural open day and a press release had been sent to the medical correspondents of newspapers. I notified the committee that I was being asked by local doctors "to put pressure on the Region to get funding for work to be done at the Horder Centre". Through personal contacts, by chance, I had arranged for Sir Roy Griffiths to address the Health Authority at Hastings on 13 September on the subject of general management and I told the committee that I would take the opportunity to speak to him about the Centre, which I did. With regard to the first patients to be admitted, 25 patients were being sent from Brighton in addition to the 200 from the Region and it was agreed that hip operations could take place at weekends if necessary. Staffing of the unit had been completed and a health authority inspection to complete registration of the surgical unit had been arranged for 13 September. The scene was set for the start of surgery.

John Ball with his Senior Management Team and Medical Wing Nurses circa 1990
Dorothy Beaumont seated far right

From the start of the surgical project a major concern to all those involved had been the long term availability of funds. The waiting list initiative was all very well as far as providing funds in the short term was concerned but no one knew for how long it would continue. As far back as January 1988, Sir Peter Baldwin, in a letter to Denys Milne, had highlighted the dilemma "From our point of view we are anxious that this proposal should make progress because this year and next year there is money available to help us ----. After that the availability of funds is unclear". The *White Paper* however, and the introduction of GP fund holding, pointed a way forward which it seemed would safeguard future funding in a way that had not existed before, although the inevitable delay while the proposed changes became established meant that interim funding would be needed for a while.

In view of these changes I decided that it would be useful for me to follow up my earlier contact with those in charge of central waiting list funds at the Department of Health to update them about our plans, in my capacity as a member of the management committee of the Centre and as the South East Thames Regional Advisor in Orthopaedic Surgery of the Royal College of Surgeons. Outlining the present position whereby the Centre had agreed to proceed, with the active support of the Regional Health Authority, with the development of a surgical unit I forecast that the first operation would take place on 28 September 1989. After further detail I summarised the situation as follows: "The difficulty facing the Horder Centre at the present time is to be able to obtain funding for the facilities which it has developed, at this stage of evolution of the NHS, whilst waiting for the proposals in the recent government *White Paper* to come into effect. The Horder Centre is in fact blazing a trail for the new form of health service provision at a time before the commissioning agencies have been fully developed. However, the Government's waiting list initiative funding allows this to be anticipated so that the problem of the over-long waiting time for hip replacement surgery can be tackled immediately". The waiting list funding could now be regarded, to use the jargon of the time, as a 'pump primer' before the full benefit of direct GP referral as enshrined in *Working for Patients* came on stream. Whether this letter had any effect is unclear but in October Vic Kempner at Region who had worked very closely with John Ball in drawing up the agreement was able to write "We are endeavouring to find more money this year but the good news is that the Department of Health has said we can fund more GP referrals direct to you".

On the 25 September 1989, 2 days before the first surgical patient was admitted, a letter addressed to John Ball was received from Dr Malcolm Forsythe to which was attached the agreement between the Centre and the Region which he and John Ball had worked so hard to achieve. Dr Forsythe was "delighted that your development is about to open its doors and wish you all every success". He went on to draw attention to the point that "since discussions began with you all several years ago, things have changed, and in particular the '*White Paper*' is clearly now in all our minds". The way was indeed opening up which would facilitate referrals directly to the Centre from a patient's fund-holding GP rather than through Region or District authorities and the Horder Centre was ready to take the lead in a new era.

Further Reading

1. Parliament. *Working for Patients*. Cmd 555. London: HMSO; 1989.

A Decade of Change
and Development

I n the final run up to the first operating session at the end of September 1989 the inevitable last minute difficulties occurred. The most troublesome of these was a demand by the inspecting authority, Eastbourne District Health Authority, for an increase in the nursing establishment. On the 13 September an inspecting team had visited the Centre to inspect the new unit and existing Centre before sending the required registration documents. These documents were duly handed over on the 22 September accompanied by a requirement that nurse staffing levels should be increased to a level, which in the view of the Centre's management team were "unjustifiably high for the level of work which we carry out". This caused a considerable problem initially in that additional staff had to be taken on at short notice. However although this was achieved the impression remained that the Authority, which had not been particularly supportive of the project from the beginning, was being unnecessarily awkward.

The first operation took place on the 28 September 1989, the patient Mr Albert Cheal of Bexhill, who had been on my waiting list at Hastings, being admitted the day before. I replaced his arthritic right hip with a Charnley type prosthesis, my surgeon assistant Nicol Stenhouse, who had worked with me since my earliest years as a consultant, assisting. Dr Colin Alexander administered the anaesthetic and Sister Carole Otway acted as theatre scrub sister. Two other patients had similar operations on the list that day. Mr Cheal made good progress and after 10 days, the normal length of time then for in-patient care, he went home. I discharged him from the follow-up clinic in early January 1990 but he remained in social contact with the Centre for many years and was a keen participant in the "Hippie Walks", which later became an important feature of fund-raising activity.

The formal opening of the surgical department took place on 25 April 1990 in the presence of the President, Her Royal Highness Princess Margaret, Countess of Snowdon.

The Princess was keenly interested in this new development at the Centre where she had always played such an active role and spent considerable time touring the new operating theatre. Sister Otway had arranged for a small display of operating instruments and prostheses to be on show and after expressing some apprehension on viewing the somewhat formidable array of orthopaedic hardware the Princess asked for an explanation of the new joints that were now being used to treat arthritis.

Dr Ivan Williams explains the function of a knee prosthesis to Princess Margaret while the designer of this particular joint looks on somewhat anxiously in case Her Royal Highness should drop it in her foot! Sister Carole Otway and John Ball stand in the foreground.

The party then moved on to the new wards where the Princess met the three patients who had had their operations six months before on the first operating list, Albert Cheal, Fred Fuller and Robert Reeves. Mr Fuller was in the unit again having had his other hip replaced the week before, the first patient at the Centre to have both hips replaced.

Princess Margaret meets Albert Cheal whilst behind him
sits Fred Fuller who had just had his second hip replaced.
Matron Gurney stands behind the Princess.

After a tour of the wards Princess Margaret asked to see the newly refurbished hydrotherapy unit that she had opened in 1986. She had asked to be kept informed about progress when she heard about the problems with the original tiling that had led to its closure for a short time and wished to see it now that it had been opened again. After this she

Princess Margaret speaks to Robert Reeves

took tea in the dining room with the residents and staff. At the end of her visit she made a private call to see Dr Peake, who was now gravely ill, an act of kindness that was appreciated not only by the staff of the Centre but especially by Joyce Peake who died a few weeks later.

Once the initial excitement of the theatre opening and the first operations had passed, attention inevitably turned towards increasing awareness of the existence of the new surgical Centre amongst the National Health Service (NHS) authorities and GPs who it was hoped would refer patients, thus reducing the long waiting time for this type of surgery. In September 1989 just before the unit opened Dr Forsythe had written to his opposite number Dr David Wild, at the South West Thames Region informing him of the new facility at Crowborough and the cost. Dr Wild's response was encouraging: "I have no doubt our Districts would be very willing to consider the Centre if the rates continue to be as competitive as they appear".

Less encouraging was the response from Brighton. In late October Mr Barry D'Arcy Fearn FRCS from Brighton, a long-standing friend of mine and Derek Richards, visited the Centre to discuss the management of the 25 patients from Brighton who it had been agreed earlier would be treated there. He was shown round by John Ball, who in a letter to his contact at Region, Vic Kempner, reported that Mr Fearn's visit "was very interesting and he felt that a lot of value could be obtained for the patients within the Brighton area with such a service". Following his visit Fearn planned to carry out a pilot operation on 22 November and "in the meantime he is going back to the unit general manager and the Director of Public Health in Brighton to advise them of his intention. I hope that this does not create a problem from your end".

Unfortunately John Ball's hope was unfounded. By return a letter was received from Brighton managers and copied to Region. A letter from the service development manager at Region, John Dennis who had now taken over from Vic Kempner, described the position with consummate tact in a letter to John Ball dated 1 November in which he wrote "In the meantime there are certain worries being expressed by them which would make pushing strongly ahead with the pilot operation rather indelicate. At its lowest I am not certain whether Brighton would be willing to pay". A great deal of time was then spent by John Ball in consultation with Barry Fearn to try and iron out the various clinical and administrative matters that were apparently a cause for concern. In the event four patients from Brighton were treated in early December but Fearn continued to experience considerable difficulty in obtaining the support he required to operate at the Centre. At the same time Derek Richards was experiencing similar problems at Eastbourne and it was not until the 21 January 1990 that he was able to start operating.

These early problems were not unexpected. We always knew there would be opposition from established organisations who inevitably saw the Centre as a threat to their well-being and indeed the NHS itself. The model of an independent hospital that was not a 'private hospital' but a Charitable Trust treating NHS patients who were not paying for their treatment as private patients was quite unknown at the time. The reluctance of some NHS establishments to use this new facility whilst perhaps understandable given its unusual character, was nonetheless the cause of some frustration in the community amongst knowledgeable lay people. In October 1990 a favourable report was received following a visit by Eastbourne Community Health Council that was in sharp contrast to its earlier critical report in 1977. "The Horder Centre package costs £1500 for all its package. The Eastbourne Health Authority considers that it can offer the same operation for £1000 and is therefore unwilling to make greater use of the Horder Centre. As the BMA estimates for this procedure £3000 we do wonder if the EHA has properly costed the complete package of treatment as it would seem that the use of the Horder Centre offers an excellent opportunity to reduce the unacceptably long orthopaedic waiting list."

The NHS had yet to take note of Sir Roy Griffiths' maxim that "the National Health Service is about delivering services to people. It is not about organising systems for their own sake". We were now looking to the GPs and the new concept of fund holding to send us the patients we had the facilities to treat and by the end of the year the first letters from that source began to arrive.

At the start a greater problem than a shortage of patients was a shortage of surgeons. It was intended in the early stages of the development that my former colleague Peter Ring would operate at the Centre. His involvement at the beginning and his moral support and expert advice throughout had been of very great benefit to us all as plans were drawn up but he was now nearing retirement and the timing was inappropriate for him to take on a new project of this magnitude. In the event he did not operate at the Centre although he and I remained in touch for some years. Barry Fearn and Derek Richards were working hard to sort out the interminable discussions with their managers on process so that they could start to operate but apart from four operations on patients from Brighton carried out by Fearn in December, operations in the first 3 months were on 36 patients of mine from Hastings. Ruth Carnall, who had recently taken over as district manager there, could not have been more supportive and we began to see a significant reduction in the number of patients waiting for joint replacement surgery at Hastings. When operating on NHS patients none of the surgeons received payment as the cost of our time, we had agreed, would be assumed to be part of our NHS contractual commitment. A similar arrangement applied to the anaesthetist and these arrangements continued until the start of the new Millennium.

On the 4 March the hundredth hip operation took place and was given prominent coverage in the *Kent & Sussex Courier*. By the time of the official opening ceremony in April we had carried out 140 operations between the three of us. However at this time it was noted that although significant numbers of patients from Hastings and in due course Eastbourne had been treated, there had been fewer referrals from Brighton and none from authorities elsewhere in the Region. In his annual report the chairman drew attention to the importance the committee attached to "extending the public awareness of the Horder Centre" and in June 1990 two orthopaedic surgeons from Tunbridge Wells, Ken Tuson and Paul Skinner, joined the three original consultants and between them carried out 32 replacements in the first year.

By the end of the first year of surgery in September 1990, 393 patients had been admitted to the Centre, of which 110 came in for medical treatment not requiring an operation. Of those admitted for surgery 242 had a hip and five a knee replacement. Thirty-nine patients under my care underwent arthroscopy of the knee, a procedure that was first introduced at the Centre in June 1990. Two other patients admitted for minor surgery made up the total. Six patients, three of whom had a joint replacement, elected to be treated as private patients, the remainder being funded by the NHS. Denys Milne's promise that the Centre would carry out 200 operations in the first year had clearly been exceeded as he had hoped.

Ten years later the figures show a significant change. There had been a four-fold increase to 1323 in the number of surgical patients admitted in the period between January and December 2000 although the number of surgeons involved was only seven, as Derek Richards had retired. However one of these, Salah Shalaby FRCS, was working full time at the Centre. A former associate specialist at Tunbridge Wells, he had been introduced to the Centre by Ken Tuson in May 1992 before taking up a full-time post there in early 1993. He worked at the Centre alongside the consultant surgeons there for more than 10 years. Two surgeons from Maidstone, Simon Ellis and Chris Walker, had also joined the team. The principal operation carried out was still either a hip or knee replacement but a broad spectrum of other orthopaedic procedures was now being introduced including a considerable amount of complex revision surgery. The number of short-stay medical in-patient admissions had dropped to 13.

In his report for the year 1993 the Medical Director, Dr Ivan Williams, noted that the "medical and surgical services have continued to expand over the past twelve months. In particular, there has been significant increase in the number of medical out-patient referrals, the majority being NHS patients referred from GP fund holding practices". With the number of patients being referred to the Centre increasing in the early 1990s as fund holding became established following the introduction of *Working for Patients*, the need for a larger out-patient department became necessary.

Fred Mountford the 1000th patient to receive a joint
replacement greets Princess Margaret

In the early days of surgery, out-patients had been seen in rooms that had been adapted from the old medical block that had existed before the surgical development. A new out-patient unit and a seminar room were opened on 20 October 1993 by Her Royal Highness Princess Margaret on the ground floor alongside the recently improved physiotherapy unit. On this occasion Her Royal Highness also met Mr Fred Mountford, the thousandth patient to have had a joint replacement at the Centre, who presented her with a bouquet of flowers. A new radiology room had also been built as the demand for X-rays had been steadily increasing and the portable apparatus that had been used in the early days of surgery was quite inadequate for the task.

By now the development of the surgical side had led Dr Williams to the view that there was a need for a Surgical Director to work alongside him and provide advice on surgical matters as well as policy and management decisions. He and John Ball asked me to take on the job, which I was willing to do, and in January 1993 the post of Surgical Director was established.

In 1995 the Committee made the decision to change the name of the Centre from the somewhat archaic "The Horder Centre for Arthritics" to the "The Horder Centre for Arthritis". Having done this it was decided to dissolve the Centre from its original governing body, The Registry of Friendly Societies, and re-register it with the Charity Commissioners as a charitable company limited by guarantee. With the agreement of Lady Dufferin, as required by the commissioners who wished to confirm that she was indeed happy for the land she had donated to be used by the new charity, this change, which had been attempted several times in the distant past was finally achieved on 28 April 1995.

In 1996 Denys Milne, after serving as Chairman for 13 years, decided to retire. During his tenure he had achieved remarkable changes taking the Centre forward from a position when it was at serious risk of closure to a point where it was able to look forward with confidence to the future. Shortly before he took over in 1983 the annual income, updated here, had been £830 000 with expenditure of £1 million leading to a deficit for the year of £170 000. When he retired, he with John Ball and his management team, had established a new independent surgical hospital providing a service for mainly NHS patients over a wide area of southern England and beyond with an annual income of £6.4 million, expenditure of £6 million and a surplus of £390 000. The buildings had been upgraded, a modern operating theatre built, a hydrotherapy pool brought into service and radiological and out-patient services introduced. Under the guidance of the two medical directors Douglas Woolf and Ivan Williams, who also retired in 1996 to be replaced by Dr Stewart Torode FRCP, new therapy units had been established and modern rehabilitation set up. 'Tiny' Milne could be well satisfied with the legacy he left the Centre.

His successor, Malcolm Forsythe FRCP, FFPHM, who had joined the committee in 1992, was the ideal candidate to take over. Having moved on from the Health Service and now working as Professor of Public Health at the University of Kent in Canterbury and as Senior Lecturer at King's College Hospital Medical School, he brought extensive experience combined with wide knowledge of the Horder Centre to the task in hand, and 1996 was to be a year of change and development at the Centre.

By now considerable numbers of patients throughout the country had received artificial joints to relieve the pain of arthritis. Inevitably some of these joints, which had been in place for many years, had become worn or loose and further surgery was required to deal with them. The Horder Centre began to see a number of such patients. Purchase of an ultrasonic device known as the Orthosonic System for Cemented Arthroplasty Revision (OSCAR), at a cost in 1996 of £33 000, provided the operating surgeon with a very useful tool to help with the removal of bone cement that had been used to fix the prosthesis in the bone at the time of the primary operation. However taking away the old prosthesis and the cement often left a large cavity and new techniques were being developed to deal with this. Custom in the past had been to fill this cavity with large quantities of bone cement but this had proved to be less than ideal. Far better was to fill the cavity with impacted bone graft, which in time became incorporated into the patient's skeleton, thus restoring the anatomy into which a new artificial joint could be fixed.

The problem initially was to obtain bone in sufficient quantities for use as a graft. Once however it was realised that bone could be used as a transplant in the way that many other organs, including blood, are used it was a relatively straightforward matter to use the bone that was routinely removed and previously discarded at the time of primary surgery, as the source of bone graft. With helpful advice from the National Blood Transfusion Service (NBTS) the necessary screening and storage facilities were set up and a bone bank was established at the Centre, one of the few pioneering units in the country to do this at that time. Bone was supplied to other hospitals on occasions. In 2001 changes in legislation led to the bone banking facility coming under the supervision of the NBTS and the Centre continued to supply bone to that organisation. In 2012 the Centre received the year's award for its contribution to the Live Bone Donation Programme presented by the NHS Blood and Transplant Service. It is of interest that when patients were asked to give their permission for the bone removed at the time of their first hip replacement to be used in this way, it was almost unknown for them to refuse and many expressed the view that they were delighted that their bone could be made available to help others.

During the course of the year a large area of the original site was landscaped to form the first therapy garden. On 25 October 1996, the thirtieth anniversary of the completion of the first building, the new garden was opened by HRH Princess Margaret. The construction of the garden was funded by two generous legacies from the estate of Mr John Cholmeley and Dr Gerhard Weiler, whose nephew attended the opening ceremony with his wife.

HRH Princess Margaret opens the new therapy garden and summer house accompanied by the Chairman, Professor Malcolm Forsythe.

Although part of the land on which this first garden was formed has been absorbed by new building developments, new gardens recently constructed between the ward blocks have drawn inspiration from this original concept of a therapy garden and seek to enhance the sense of well-being of the patients as they regain their mobility following surgery. Phase two of the recent development project started in 2010 included plans for the creation of these gardens with quiet seating areas, smooth and level walking surfaces and planting to encourage birds and other wildlife. These gardens will be within easy access of the patients' rooms and the first was completed in autumn 2011. A project to create three outdoor activity trails in the grounds is now also underway.

When she came to open the original therapy garden Her Royal Highness came to stay with her friends the Earl and Countess De La Warr at Buckhurst Park, Withyam and as she had arrived by helicopter the Chief Executive was asked to provide a car to bring the Princess to the Centre. Fortunately the Surgical Director was able to provide a suitable vehicle of an appropriate colour and the police driver had an unusual experience driving a classic Bentley!

Dark clouds however were on the horizon. With an act of supreme political foolishness the incoming Government in 1997 abolished GP fund holding thus extinguishing at a stroke the goodwill of scores of doctors who had worked hard to improve their practices and who were beginning to bring real pressure to bear on the hospitals to improve their services. The chairman, Professor Forsythe, in his report in 1998 describing the Centre's partnership with the NHS drew attention to the problem. After acknowledging that the New Labour Government in its pre-election rhetoric in 1997 had promised a reduction in NHS waiting lists together with encouragement of a partnership between the public and private sectors, which seemed to be exactly what the Centre wanted, he described the situation as he saw it. "In practice the NHS has been struggling to reinstate financial control, thus increasing waiting lists and creating spare capacity. The government's current priority therefore is to see NHS facilities used to the maximum before recourse to the private sector." The new Secretary of State for Health, Frank Dobson, in an attempt to stop all NHS treatment in private hospitals, instigated a policy whereby the names of all NHS patients treated in "private hospitals" had to be reported to him although he appeared to be unaware that the definition 'private hospital' included charitable as well as commercial organisations. As a consequence of this policy the Centre was prevented from providing services for NHS patients as it had been doing in the era of GP fund holding and John Ball was forced to undertake an extensive mailing campaign, with visits to former GP fund holders and their practice managers together with hospital commissioning managers, to attract patients. Those who could afford to pay for their treatment, either through insurance or their own resources were treated, until the ever-increasing waiting list for joint replacement surgery in the NHS and a change of policy introduced by the Minister of State, Alan Milburn, who was to take over eventually as Secretary of State, led to a more pragmatic approach. As the Chairman put it in his report: "The reality is that the NHS has not the capacity in terms of staff as well as facilities to deliver its targets for waiting list patients. This, together with pressure from general practitioners who hold the [Centre] in high regard, has now resulted in a return to our normal referral rate". He went on "I can only reiterate that the committee of management will always regard The Horder Centre for Arthritis as being in partnership with the NHS. Our ability to deliver a good quality surgical service was achieved with financial help from the NHS and the secondment of orthopaedic and anaesthetic specialists from local trusts to treat their NHS patients in our Centre. ---- Long may this partnership continue".

With these few succinct words the Chairman neatly summarised the philosophy behind the surgical development from its beginning to the present day. Inevitably the reduction in patient referrals led to a fall in net incoming resources and this amounted to around 86 percent from £243 500 in 1997 to £32 000 in 1998. This combined with a sharp decline in voluntary donations and an increase in direct expenditure on patient services meant that the committee had to re-think the fund-raising strategy for the coming year. Nevertheless the early downturn in patient admissions, which followed the abolition of fund-holding debacle of 1997, was soon reversed by pressure from patients and their GPs. However it provided a warning of difficult times ahead for both the Centre and the NHS as the new millennium came into view.

A New Millennium

At the Annual General Meeting (AGM) on 22 July 1999 Professor Forsythe retired as Chairman and handed over to Sir Tim Chessells KBE, although he agreed to remain as a trustee. Sir Tim, with his great experience in the City, combined with a wide knowledge of the National Health Service (NHS) and health services acquired during his time as Chairman of the North East Thames Regional Health Authority and as Chairman of the Guy's and St Thomas' Charitable Foundation, in addition to many other such positions, brought his skills to bear on the Centre's work at a time when it was again battling with an unfavourable financial climate yet was poised to move forward into a new era. The Centre had again been fortunate to find another distinguished leader to take on the office of Chairman at that time.

Sadly one of his early duties was to announce the sudden and unexpected death of the former Chairman, Denys Milne, on 9 February 2000. Many of us from the Centre attended the funeral service at St Michael and All Angels at Withyham nearby. A few months after this in October the death of the former Medical Director, Douglas Woolf was also announced.

When Sir Tim took over, the income of the Centre was £6 million* and this rose to £6.6 million in the following year providing an operating surplus, which combined with interest on investments and charitable donations amounted to

---

* Figures adjusted for inflation as at 2012.

approximately £700 000, providing funds for much needed further development and he was quick to seize the opportunity. The most pressing requirement was for a larger out-patient department as the steady increase in the number of joint replacements had led to a parallel rise in the number of out-patient attendances. By the year 2000 more than 6000 major joint replacements had been carried out together with over 3300 other orthopaedic procedures and there was an urgent need for another re-development and enlargement of the out-patient department as well as other areas.

In January 2000 tenders were invited from construction companies to build the new department and in April John Ball told the committee that after discussion with the Vice-Chairman Mr Anthony Chapman, Westbridge Construction Ltd of Bodiam East Sussex had been appointed builders. Some delay occurred when it became necessary to remove old asbestos tiles from the original building but by the autumn the out-patient department together with an adjacent radiology room had been completed on time and new equipment installed.

The new department was opened by HRH Princess Margaret on 27 October 2000 on what was to be her twelfth and last visit to the Horder Centre. We all knew that she had not been well but in spite of this she inspired all those who met her with her interest in their work and the notice she took of the progress that had been made at the establishment of which she had been President for more than 40 years.

It was with great sadness that not long after this last visit, on 9 February 2002, it was announced that Princess Margaret had died. The Horder Centre had the privilege of being able to send representatives to the Memorial Service held at Westminster Abbey on 19 April 2002 and five of us attended. Those who had met her at the Centre on many occasions over the years would remember her as a warm and compassionate person whose dedication to her duties as President brought encouragement to both staff and patients alike. She has been much missed and the office of President, which she filled with such distinction, remains vacant still.

In April 2001, towards the end of his term of office, John Ball told the committee that the discussions he had been having with a number of consultant anaesthetists regarding setting up a consultant-led anaesthetic service at the Centre had reached a conclusion. Dr Colin Alexander FFARCS, who had recently retired from the NHS at Hastings, would take up duties on a regular basis in early September and would lead the anaesthetic department for the next 5 years. Dr Robin Loveday FFARCS from Tunbridge Wells would work regularly at the Centre on Fridays. It was hoped that three other anaesthetists would become involved and provide assistance in out-patients and advice on post-operative pain control. Dr Tom Price and Dr Jan MacDonald who had given loyal service since the start of the surgical project would retire and Professor Forsythe arranged for gifts in recognition of their service to be presented to them both on behalf of the committee in September, when the new arrangements would begin.

At the AGM in July 2001 the Chairman paid tribute to John Ball who had retired at the beginning of July after serving as Chief Executive for 13 years. Since he had come to the Centre in 1988 the income from fees on which future development depended had increased seven-fold. When he arrived he took on the task of introducing and developing surgery at the Centre. Conversion of outdated buildings into surgical wards, overseeing building and commissioning of the new operating theatre and re-training of staff were just some of the tasks that confronted him. He took the Centre forward into a completely new era at a time when it was struggling to survive. He turned what was in effect an act of faith on the part of all concerned into a burgeoning reality. In the Chairman's words: "He has given wonderful service to the Centre through these years, seen the evolution to a major joint replacement centre and has led the Centre's developments with skill and energy. John goes with the thanks of all the trustees and the management committee, who all wish him a happy and fulfilling retirement".

The new Chief Executive, Diane Thomas MBA, RGN, took up her post on 2 July 2001. She had been managing the Nuffield Health Group in

Nottingham since 1995 and had previously worked as matron and operations manager of Ramsey Healthcare UK. She had also managed a number of other charity hospitals. Expansion, improvement and modernisation perhaps best characterises the new era for the Horder Centre that she introduced.

In March 2000 during discussions on the budget for the year 2000/2001, I had expressed the view that the present facilities within the theatre suite and surgical wards were nearing the limit of their capacity. Having as it were "got her feet under the table" Diane Thomas announced in the *Spring 2002 Newsletter* her plans to build a new surgical wing. The original theatre, which had been state of the art at the time it was built, was beginning to reach the stage where it would fall outside the guidelines and requirements of current legislation, particularly with regard to its size. Upgrading the old theatre was impractical at that time as it would mean that surgery would have to shut down for nine months whilst the building work was carried out. It was decided therefore to build an entirely new surgical complex linked to the main building by a corridor, which would include a twin operating theatre suite. In addition a new reception area was designed leading to the out-patient and therapy departments and the wards. Major improvements were also to be carried out to the resident's facilities. A major appeal was launched in 2002 to raise the £2.5 million needed to pay for all this work and by the time the theatre was opened £1.14 million had already been raised

The new theatre suite was opened for the first operation on 31 March 2003 when Ken Tuson carried out a joint replacement with Dr Colin Alexander administering the anaesthetic just as he had when Mr Albert Cheal, the first patient to be operated on at the Centre had had his hip replaced in September 1989. The opening of the new theatre was celebrated

THE HORDER CENTRE

news spring 2004

50 YEARS AND STILL GOING STRONG!

The Horder Centre set amidst the beautiful Ashdown Forest

"2004 is another very exciting year in the history of The Horder Centre. 50 years ago this year the Charity was first registered and it has achieved many major landmarks along the way.

Rather than harping-on about our very successful past, I'd just like to cover a few points about what the future has in store for us and our patients.

Our policy of continuous improvement means we are constantly striving to ensure that The Horder Centre is an enjoyable experience in many ways.

Our Executive Team recognises the strength of our workforce and that the Centre's success is dependent upon keeping its staff well-trained and motivated to deliver excellent patient care. My sincere thanks go out to all our staff for the continuing major contributions that they make towards our success.

Completion of our state-of-the-art theatres and extensive refurbishment programme, combined with our highly skilled consultant surgeons and theatre teams, mean that our patients benefit from the most advanced facilities available, and literally enjoy speedy recoveries.

The number of letters I receive from patients that are full of praise for what we provide and the way we provide it, are testament to this and are a tremendous source of satisfaction to the Centre.

Things just seem to keep on getting better and better at The Horder Centre, and it is with tremendous enthusiasm that we face the challenges ahead. So whatever those challenges might be, we are confident that with our special brand of patient care and our state-of-the-art facilities, we will be ready to provide the very best for our patients for the next 50 years."

Hydrotherapy Pool

State-of-the-Art Operating Theatre

Di Thomas — Chief Executive

in the *The Horder Centre News* spring edition in 2004. The picture on the front of the newsletter showed an aerial view of the new theatre complex at the bottom of the buildings in the foreground with a view of the interior of one of the operating theatres at the bottom of the page alongside the hydrotherapy pool. Later that year I decided that the time had come for me to 'hang up the knife' and retire from clinical practice and I handed over the surgical directorship to my colleague Ken Tuson. The Committee of Management acting on the advice of the Chief Executive did me the very great honour of naming the new theatre block *The Gallannaugh Suite*.

It was now 60 years since Cecilia Bochenek had first registered her Horder Centres for Arthritics with the Registrar of Friendly Societies thus starting a chain of events that led to the Horder Healthcare of today. It is unlikely that she would have foreseen all the clinical and social changes that have occurred over the past half century but from what we know of her it seems likely that she would have approved of the Centre in its modern form. The purpose of joint replacement surgery is to relieve pain and restore independence so that patients can resume their place in society exactly as Bochenek had described when she laid down the original aims of her organisation. The demand for long-term residential care however, which was very much a feature in the early years, gradually declined, as changes in society and the medical management of arthritis moved the emphasis from residential to community care. Gradually the number of residents dwindled until finally only four remained and in 2006 the residents' unit was closed, the last few patients moving to nursing homes.

Perhaps in the years ahead this story of the development of an independent hospital working in partnership with the NHS will be taken further as others look back to 2012 taking advantage of the perspective that time provides. To celebrate the recent multi-million pound re-development scheme, in November 2011 local dignitaries including the Mayor of Crowborough, Councillor Kay Moss and school children from nearby schools came to the Centre to bury a time capsule alongside the Gwen Balchin memorial tree. It is intended to open it in 50 years time when perhaps some of those young children who helped bury it will set eyes on it once again accompanied by their own children or grandchildren. The record it contains will no doubt be of great interest to historians in the future.

Many changes have taken place in the 10 years since the new theatre suite was opened. The original operating theatre and surrounding area were rebuilt and replaced by a modern operating suite for the treatment of patients requiring day surgery. The emergent clinical governance systems, which the Medical Director Dr Stewart Torode and the senior nurse manager Lene Gurney pioneered in 2000, together with systems of clinical audit, have been built on and developed into sophisticated management tools in tandem with those that have been introduced in the NHS.

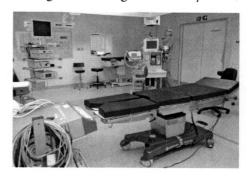

The appointment of a data analysis expert, Stephanie Kiryluk, who worked closely with Lene Gurney, meant that data analysis became an essential component of the audit process with all joint replacement data being submitted to the National Joint Registry. In 2012 the Dr Foster Guide, an independent annual report that details improvements and trends across the healthcare sector, included details from independent providers for the first time. The Horder Centre was named as one of the country's best providers thanks to the consistently high-quality outcomes that it had been able to demonstrate, a tremendous reward for the work of everyone who works at the Centre in whatever capacity.

In 2010, as part of a Government initiative, a new contract *Any Qualified Provider* was signed between the Horder Centre and the South East Coast Strategic Health Authority, the Centre being the first independent healthcare provider in the South East to be awarded this new contract to treat NHS patients. The contract that came into effect on the 1 April 2011 enabled the Centre to provide services for the NHS for orthopaedic surgery, pain services and rheumatology. Over 90% of the Centre's work is carried out for the NHS and it also provides high-quality orthopaedic and musculo-skeletal treatment for patients who are privately insured or who wish to fund their own care. Maintaining and developing the symbiotic relationship between the Centre and other groups of NHS providers of health care as well as forging new relationships with the GP commissioning groups of the future, thus putting emphasis on the successful business model on which the Centre is established, will dominate executive thinking in the years ahead.

On 27 September 2011 the Olympic athlete Sally Gunnell OBE opened the new state of the art physiotherapy department. Now our physiotherapists, as well as treating those recovering from their orthopaedic operations, will

provide musculo-skeletal services to sports clubs and all those who are seeking help with sports-related injuries, opening up a new market for the Centre at a time when the recent very successful London Olympics have provided the background, it is hoped, for a revival of interest in sport amongst all ages. Recently outreach physiotherapy services have been opened in Eastbourne at the Apollo Centre, part of the Princes Park Health Centre and at Hookwood near Reigate, in Surrey. Many patients who receive treatment at the Centre in Crowborough come from these areas and by providing local service in this way patients are given easier access to follow-up care. The service also enables the staff of the Centre to monitor outcomes following surgery more closely. More such developments are planned for the future.

The recent capital re-development programme included a new entrance and reception area with refurbished communal areas and more *en suite*

patient rooms. A new admissions suite has been built together with a new day care centre and pre-admission assessment clinic. Writing in the annual report for 2011/2012 Diane Thomas summarised the achievements of the past 12 months. "The redevelopment programme has not only enabled us to improve our outcomes for patients but also to deliver new services to an even wider audience, all based on the same high level of quality and care that we are committed to. I am encouraged by the very positive feedback we have received, a clear indication that the redevelopment has made a real impact on our patients and staff."

In 2009 Sir Tim Chessells retired as Chairman after nine years although after a short break he returned to the Board as a director and continues to provide his forthright and much valued advice. Now under the guidance of the present Chairman, Roy Greenhalgh, with Diane Thomas and her executive team ever looking for new challenges, The Horder Centre can look forward to the future with confidence and excitement ever mindful of the fact that it exists solely to deliver high-quality health care to those in need of its services. That quest for quality will continue to predominate over all its actions and thinking.

From the patient's perspective, whilst taking for granted that they will receive the best clinical treatment, what matters is that they are looked after with compassion by people who care. To them it is the nurses and front-of-house staff who deliver that care and when patients are asked how they fared in the Centre it is commonplace for them to comment on the wonderful attention they received from the nursing and other staff. Sir Lancelot may deliver miracles of modern surgery, but to the anxious patient it is the nurses and all the staff of the Centre "who were so kind and really cared for me in the hospital" who really matter. It is a lesson that many in today's NHS need to learn again.

Speaking at the NHS Confederation Conference in 2012, the Centre's Chief Executive Diane Thomas described the importance that the staff of the Centre places on listening to patients, using feedback questionnaires, face-to-face interviews, daily ward rounds by Matron and random impromptu surveys using iPads and patient focus groups. She pointed out that "the positive behaviours which patients value don't cost a lot. It is the way things are done that really matter and that can deliver exceptional patient experience. Our values are clearly aligned to the types of behaviours patients want to experience and a caring ethos is embedded in our culture".

The long serving clinical staff of the Horder Centre in 2012
The Resident Medical Officer Dr Isam El Haj stands back row second right

The Horder Centre has come a long way since the day in 1966 when Cecilia Bochenek and Dr Peake published their annual report for that year. At that time the gross income, as at today's prices, was £940 000 of which £17 000 had been derived from patient income, the remainder being obtained from fund raising activity or charitable donations. Unfortunately it is not possible to obtain accurate figures for the number of admissions each year from the surviving records but it was clearly less than 100. In 2011 there were 2233 patients admitted as in-patients of whom 1661 had a hip or knee joint replaced. There were 2274 day cases and almost 25 000 patients were seen in the out-patient clinics. The four surgeons who had carried out the first few operations in 1989/1990 had been replaced by 17, together with their attendant anaesthetists and the Medical Director Dr Paul Reynolds is supported by three other consultant physicians. The net income published in the Annual Report was almost £5 million. When questionnaires were sent recently to 5500 patients, 65% were returned and 99% of patients reported their experience of the Centre as excellent or very good. The same number said they were treated with dignity and respect at all times and would recommend the Centre.

In June 2011 the Horder Centre had the distinction of being praised by the Prime Minister, David Cameron. In a speech to NHS staff in which he drew attention to the ways in which independent providers can help to raise standards and provide competition by giving a "mixed economy of providers", he referred to "the independent Horder Centre in East Sussex, which delivers orthopaedic care and has high patient satisfaction, low rates of readmission and excellent outcomes". The Horder Centre staff could not have put it better themselves.

EPILOGUE

In 1959 I, then a medical student at St Thomas' Hospital, sat at the bedside of my mother who was a patient there. She was dying but we kept up the pretence to each other, as people who are very close do in such circumstances, that it would not be long before she would feel better as the radiotherapy treatment helped to ease the pain of bone cancer. She was in a room at the side of the main Nightingale ward and it was peaceful. There was an air of order and discipline in the ward. The flowers that she had received and which gave her much pleasure were carefully arranged each day by the ward orderly and they chatted together while this task was carried out. From time to time when I was there a nurse, sometimes a very senior nurse, would come in "just to see if there is anything you want". I was senior enough to know that when she was moved it had to be done with great skill if she was not to suffer severe pain and I asked her one day if she was being well looked after. She answered without hesitation and I remember her words. "I cannot fault the care I receive from the nurses and everyone else here. This is a wonderful hospital. You will be able to learn so much while you are here from watching the way they care for us."

Fifty years later in 2011 I stood at the bedside of another family member in a district general hospital on the south coast. He also was at the end of his life, unable to stand, almost blind because of a secondary tumour in the back of his brain and too weak to carry out the simple tasks of everyday life without assistance. When we visited him we usually found him sitting in a chair by the side of the bed, often in discomfort, the catheter he required blocked so that it leaked allowing a pool to develop on the floor around his slippers. A cold cup of tea often remained on top of the locker on the opposite side of the bed, unseen and out of reach. At intervals a shriek rent the air from a poor individual in a bed nearby as his dementia took hold again and his elderly wife, in almost as much distress as he, did her best unaided, to calm him. Nursing assistants if seen at all seemed to have little understanding of their tasks and dignity and respect for the patient appeared to be absent. I felt at times as though I was viewing a painting by Hogarth except there was no gin to bring solace. The concept of compassionate care was clearly absent or unknown. In due course we were able to rescue him and he died not long after in a private nursing home nearby where he received the exemplary care in his last days, which should be the right of anyone in such circumstances in a civilised society.

In the 50 years between these two events something has gone terribly wrong with the National Health Service (NHS). The National Health Service has, it could be said, become the National Health Shambles. It is now commonplace to read of some disaster or other occurring either to an individual or to a whole hospital population. Numerous studies take place most of which conclude with serious criticism of a failing service. Investigations of the most notorious cases take place and the eventual report usually ends with the futile comment "it must never happen again". A week later it does. It would have been inconceivable 50 years ago for a young man to die, as reported recently, in the very ward of a great London teaching hospital where I once practised as a consultant orthopaedic surgeon, of dehydration caused by previously diagnosed diabetes insipidus, in the presence of his mother who had apparently tried desperately to obtain treatment for him. How can a system of care in which two hospitals in Surrey discharge more than 1000 elderly patients between 11 pm and 6 am over a 3-year period be considered 'fit for purpose'. Yet every enquiry that highlights yet another disaster is met with an outburst of denial or as in the case quoted above attracts some oleaginous platitude. In this case, according to the *Daily Telegraph*,[1] which extracted the information with a freedom of information request, the explanation was that "the numbers represented only about two percent of discharges". The 1000 vulnerable patients who were sent out into the night, 98 of whom were over 90 years old, were clearly no more than a blip in the statistics in the overall scheme of things.

There is no doubt that at its best, usually in the highly technical arena, the NHS provides a very high standard of care and great medical advances have brought enormous benefit to countless numbers of patients. Many tens of thousands of hard-working doctors and nurses together with supporting staff, without whose efforts hospitals and surgeries would not function, work to deliver the best possible care they can. But they work in spite of the system often without its support and many give up the unequal struggle. The NHS today is no longer regarded by the majority of patients as a great organisation. It is tolerated because no one so far has been able to introduce a way to improve it and it is a strong-minded politician indeed who dares to challenge it in his own constituency however abysmal the service it delivers locally may be. In many NHS units as we read regularly in the newspapers the level of care is mediocre and in the worst, atrocious.

When, in the early 1960s, I and my fellow students climbed onto the first rung of the medical ladder and took up our house jobs, the fact that we were working within the NHS meant almost nothing to us. We identified with our own hospital, St Thomas's, which as far as we were concerned was the best and we strove to maintain the high standard of care inherited from our forbears. The huge bureaucratic juggernaut of the NHS was something for others to grapple with and seemed to have little to do with our own beloved hospital. People do not identify with vast monolithic structures where innovation and individual achievement is stifled. When organisations are broken down into manageable units in which individual leaders are able to inspire then great things are possible.

Such parochialism is unwelcome to many politicians. At election time being able to refer to the "envy of the world" or "our wonderful NHS" provides a far better sound bite than a vague reference to the improvements in the care of the elderly that came about as a result of the sheer hard work of a group of nurses at a hospital somewhere in the north. The fact that nowhere has anyone sought to establish a similarly enviable organisation is quietly omitted in the euphoria of electioneering. Attempts to micromanage from the centre such a huge organisation in its present form are doomed to failure and only by breaking it down into smaller parts can meaningful control be re-established. Granting autonomy to individual units be they hospital or community based could do much to re-establish pride and self-esteem in a workforce that is clearly demoralised today.

Examples already exist that demonstrate that the one-size-fits-all model is outdated. The recent concentration of cardiac surgery in a reduced number of units each with a larger throughput of patients where surgical expertise can be enhanced is a step forward. Similarly the orthopaedic hospital at Wrightington in Lancashire or the Horder Centre in Sussex demonstrate how high-quality joint replacement surgery can be provided by both the NHS and the independent sector when skilled specialist care is concentrated. The management of strokes by concentrating expertise in a few specialised units with full back-up facilities, as developed in London by Dame Ruth Carnall and her team at NHS London, has changed the outlook for large numbers of patients previously devastated by this common and crippling condition. The concentration of specialists at the Queen Elizabeth Hospital in Birmingham to deal with casualties from Afghanistan is clearly better than a plethora of old military hospitals scattered around the country each with limited resources and expertise. As is already recognised modern accident and emergency surgery needs around-the-clock, across-specialty, consultant-led care to be effective. The technical support required to administer high-quality treatment cannot be provided in every small local hospital or district general hospital. When *The Mail on Sunday*[2] recently reported an interview with the President of the Royal College of Surgeons, who had commented on the proposed closure of many smaller accident centres around the country, pointing out the truth known to every experienced surgeon that creating specialist 'centres of excellence' would force patients to travel further but would increase the provision of high-quality care and their chances of survival, he was immediately accused in an accompanying editorial of treating patients as guinea pigs. "No one working for the NHS, at whatever level, should ever forget their first duty of care is to them (the patients)" the paper thundered, which is indeed precisely what the President was trying to point out. Such changes in practice will always raise howls of anguish from those who hold entrenched positions, often but not exclusively from those on the left of the political spectrum. Such conflict has to be overcome if the population as a whole is to be enabled to access modern high-quality clinical care.

In the present and future economic climate the voracious appetite of the NHS, as it is now set up, to absorb money to maintain many obsolete practices becomes less and less sustainable. Attempts to carry on with this monolithic relic of the past in its present form and require it to provide an acceptable standard of health care for the population of this country have been shown to be unworkable. The 'guinea pigs' the media refers to have already been subjected to the experiment. Action on the results of that 60-year-old experiment is now needed. Those who pretend that it can continue in its more or less original form, albeit with minor adjustments, are doing little more than perpetrating fraud upon the people. A state monopoly is no longer tenable. A radical change is needed and if the independent sector of health care or the private sector can assist their contribution should be welcomed. The Horder Centre at Crowborough has shown that the independent sector working in partnership with the NHS can provide a very high quality of surgical care, still free for patients at the point of delivery.

Speaking at a conference organised by the think tank Reform in 2012[3] to discuss what had become known as the 'Nicholson Challenge' of making efficiency savings of between £15 billion and £20 billion before 2014, the Chairman of the Commons Health Select Committee and former Secretary of State for Health, the Rt Hon Stephen Dorrell MP was quoted as saying that he believed the challenge could only be met by a fundamental rethink. "We have to begin again. ----. The institutions of 1948 are not appropriate to today's patients. Why are we stuck with community care and primary care, which do the same job? It's the result of a deal Nye Bevan struck in 1948, and every single person involved in that deal is now dead."

In these words he described clearly the present challenge facing managers, politicians and the professions alike who are faced with the task of providing health care for the people of this country. Change is needed and the independent Horder Healthcare of today has demonstrated that there is indeed another way.

Further Reading

1. Elderly discharged at midnight. *The Daily Telegraph*. 26 July 2012.

2. Chief Surgeon Backs Axing of A&E wards, by Jo Macfarlane, medical correspondent. *The Mail on Sunday*. 12 August 2012, p30.

3. Nigel Hawkes. BMJ 2012; 344: e4175.

INDEX

Lightning Source UK Ltd.
Milton Keynes UK
UKOW050414260613

212804UK00002B/137/P